Uncommon Leadership

Erik —
with best wishes
for your leadership
journey!

Debbie

Uncommon Leadership

Live Well, Lead Strong
for Courage and Integrity

Debbie McFalone, PhD

ROWMAN & LITTLEFIELD
Lanham • Boulder • New York • London

Published by Rowman & Littlefield
An imprint of The Rowman & Littlefield Publishing Group, Inc.
4501 Forbes Boulevard, Suite 200, Lanham, Maryland 20706
www.rowman.com

6 Tinworth Street, London SE11 5AL

British Library Cataloguing in Publication Information Available

Library of Congress Cataloging-in-Publication Data Available

ISBN: 978-1-4758-4556-3 (cloth : alk. paper)
ISBN: 978-1-4758-4557-0 (pbk. : alk. paper)
ISBN: 978-1-4758-4558-7 (electronic)

∞™ The paper used in this publication meets the minimum requirements of American National Standard for Information Sciences—Permanence of Paper for Printed Library Materials, ANSI/NISO Z39.48-1992.

Printed in the United States of America

With a heart full of love,
this book is dedicated to
Sofia, Nico, and Seeley . . .
uncommon young people,
Uncommon Leaders of the future.

Contents

List of Figures

List of Tables

Preface

This is a book about strong leadership—strategies, ideas, and stories about the everyday actions of today's Uncommon Leaders that enable them to live well and to lead strong. It's about leaders who cultivate habits of reflective thinking and intentional action, and who are leaving a positive legacy of courage and integrity in their organizations.

Some of these stories are grounded in my own experience as an educational leader, but most come from the hundreds of leaders with whom I've worked over the last several years.

I recently held a coaching conversation with a very talented early-career principal who had received some great feedback from her teachers about her first year in leadership. "Kristen's taken a good school and made us even better," one teacher remarked on her feedback survey form. Other teachers mentioned Kristen's transparency, fairness in making decisions, grace under pressure, and knowledge of excellent teaching. An experienced fifth grade teacher signed her lovely note: #bestprincipalever. How wonderful!

Wonderful . . . and yet here's the reality check: Although Kristen was excited and pleased to receive so many positive comments about her work, she knew that many times during the school year she felt drained and exhausted by the stressors so abundant in the principalship today. "I know I can do this job," Kristen shared with me, "I'm just not sure for how long."

That authentic comment from a young leader brought me up short. *What kind of schools are we shaping today, where our most talented people are feeling so depleted and unable to maintain their strength and energy as leaders?*

That question was a challenge to me and spurred my thinking, leading me to write this book.

It's my hope that the strategies, examples, and ideas within this book will be helpful to Kristen and to the hundreds of other leaders who feel exactly the same way. In these chapters, we'll focus on how superintendents, central office people, and principals can maintain that vibrant positivity that permeates their schools—the direct result of being "plugged in" to their own deeply held values and then acting in alignment with those guiding principles every day.

A FEAR-BASED CULTURE

As part of my work, I visit a great number of schools each year, stepping into classrooms with district and school leaders and visiting with them and with the teachers about the learning we see. In doing this work, I have noticed that *a fear-based culture permeates our schools today, and it's a significant barrier to learning for our adults and for our students.*

Fearful superintendents are worried that their decisions will be second-guessed, that their board meetings will become chaotic and filled with protesters, and that the media will examine every decision with a laser-like, microscopic, judgmental lens. These fears, coupled with a fear that state bureaucrats will penalize them for any misstep, often paralyze timid leaders. In the very worst cases, it's as though these superintendents have had their spines surgically removed!

At the same time, fearful principals are afraid of parents who feel free to use social media to damage educators' professional reputations and of teachers who use gossip and mean-spirited actions to squelch collaboration in their schools.

And our teachers? Those enthusiastic, gifted adults who entered the profession with a clear sense of moral purpose, wanting to change the lives of their students? Those teachers are now scared stiff of being ranked, sorted, judged, criticized, and found wanting due to the abusive misuse of evaluation checklists and shallow processes that, when used in isolation, never impact learning in classrooms and, in my experience, are a waste of time for us all.

What's more, teachers fear being "blamed and shamed" in a toxic culture of competition. They resist sharing their best ideas with others and certainly never approach a colleague for help when they're struggling. The end result? In those schools, our students never have the benefit of teachers who experience the safety net of supportive teacher-colleagues or of a principal or district leader focused on coaching them for improvement. Of course the students are struggling—because the adults are struggling!

This culture of fear is a significant barrier to the innovative thinking our students need to succeed in today's world and it damages all of us in the education arena. Schools filled with anxious, tense, resentful, and frustrated adults will never be places of productive, joyful learning where children are challenged and cherished . . . and we need to do something about that.

POINTS OF HOPE

I do visit schools where I see positive and productive, rather than fear-filled, work being guided by skillful leaders. The masterful leaders I know refuse to be controlled by the fear that permeates our culture today. Instead . . .

Superintendents are transparent in their decision-making, their communication, and their adherence to their guiding principles in everything they do. They have deep knowledge about current best practices to foster innovation, they realize the power of gratitude and appreciation, and they are committed to supporting risk-taking and removing the fear of failure.

Principals build bridges to connect with parents. They nurture trust with teachers through their competence, approachability, and warmth, and through the care they exhibit for the students and for the adults in their schools.

Teachers feel a balance of support and accountability from their leaders— support that focuses on coaching and providing resources and a sense of accountability that motivates and drives them to continually seek professional growth. These teachers experience the power of collaborative work with other teachers and the innovation and creativity that comes from shared ideas.

These Uncommon Leaders refuse to allow a culture of fear to enter the process of teacher evaluation. They view the evaluation process as a growth opportunity grounded in dialogue, rather than a hierarchical model of old thinking involving the inauthentic leader who pontificates a judgment from on high about a teacher's performance. They are deeply involved in the *adaptive* work of holding rich conversations with teachers about their practice.

Uncommon Leaders offer ideas, serve as sounding boards, connect people to resources, and firmly hold all their people accountable to one standard of excellence across their districts.

Where does that type of skillful leadership come from? It's deeply rooted in the leaders' firm knowledge about who they are, what they believe about impactful leadership, and their practice of acting in alignment with that knowledge every day.

Never before have we had such a need for reflective, intentional, courageous leaders in our schools. As James Kouzes and Barry Posner remind us in their 2016 book *Learning Leadership*, during times of change, "adversity and uncertainty characterize every personal best leadership experience" (8)—and they're absolutely right! We need Uncommon Leadership now, and it's critical for leaders to own the power they have in order to shape the future for our students.

Our leaders today face daunting barriers to their success, but they also have the opportunity to become stronger and more skilled than they've ever believed possible. We've never known more about effective instruction, about diverse learners, and about the collaborative culture so needed in our schools today. We know a great deal about exemplary leadership and about the emotional intelligence and positivity that leaders need to bring to their work today—we just need to commit, now, to putting those ideas into practice!

It's my hope that this book will help leaders build their capacity for maintaining personal and professional strength—helping them become Uncommon Leaders, living well through reflection and intentionality, and leading strong through their commitment to be courageous and trustworthy.

I believe that's the secret to skillful leadership, and guess what? It's available to anyone who's committed to growing and learning! So, let's get started.

REFERENCES

Kouzes, J., and Posner, B. 2010. *The Truth about Leadership: The No-fads, Heart-of-the-Matter Facts You Need to Know*. San Francisco, CA: Jossey-Bass.

Acknowledgments

I'm very grateful to Tom Koerner and the Rowman & Littlefield organization, for offering me this opportunity in my first publishing venture. Copy editor Pat George has been a godsend, and her eye for detail and form has made the book immeasurably better.

I've had the great good fortune to be surrounded by lifelong loving relationships and support for my life and work. In that spirit, I'm deeply thankful for my parents, whose legacy of faith, integrity, courage, and unconditional love shaped my life and the lives of my siblings. Miriam, Bill, and Karey are Uncommon Leaders in their own right.

My husband Brian offers energy and a strong belief in me that never wavers, and models listening as the highest form of love. His solid presence is a rock for me, and his care for me is a gift I treasure.

My wonderful educator daughters, Meghan and Kristen, bless me daily by sharing their keen insight, their straightforward perspective and their own stories of courage in their lives. I'm so grateful to our daughter Mairi for all her support and care from across the miles!

My niece, Miriam Bonano, gifts me each week by taking one of my leadership quotes and designing it into a graphic for posting on social media. I'm so thankful for her many talents!

I'm incredibly grateful for my exemplary teaching partner, Derek Wheaton, whose unbounded enthusiasm for leadership is a model for us all. Paul Liabenow, executive director of the Michigan Elementary and Middle School Principals Association, has offered unconditional support, a keen perspective, and support for me as a person as well as a leader. Thank you so much!

The hundreds of school leaders who have been part of my learning sessions have greatly enriched my understanding of skillful leadership in today's schools. Their courage, creativity, and commitment to the future generation truly fill me with awe. Make no mistake: our children are in capable, compassionate hands. I'm so filled with hope when I consider the talent and creativity of all the leaders with whom I work!

Finally, to the many women who have for years been my friends of the heart . . . your encouragement and care mean the world to me. I'm "standing on your shoulders," and I thank you.

Introduction

What if leaders in organizations far and wide were willing to be *learners,* committed to continuously growing in their capacity to lead? What if they had the will to develop the skills needed to become thoughtful, intentional, courageous people who bring out the best in those around them?

What would it be like if every day, people all over the world went to work and were inspired and valued by these leaders? We'll call them Uncommon Leaders—those whose leadership is built on a foundation of self-knowledge, courage, and integrity. Their effect on those around them is wonderful to see.

These exemplary leaders share two universal characteristics that enable them to perform effectively and to leave a legacy of productivity and positivity in their organizations. These two characteristics form the structure and organization of this book.

First, Uncommon Leaders are deeply grounded in their values and guiding principles—in short, they "live well." They intentionally cultivate habits of reflection and mindfulness that keep them in touch with their beliefs and promote personal and professional growth.

Second, Uncommon Leaders have courage and integrity that flow from that foundation. Their actions align with their beliefs as they "lead strong."

Uncommon Leadership is forged through the combination of the leaders' commitment to knowing their truth and living their truth. This book offers ideas, strategies, and experiences from leaders to support your learning and growth in both areas.

Each chapter highlights an element that is key to successful leadership and provides readers with foundational thoughts and experiences related to the ideas, as well as strategies to adapt the learning and make it relevant to their own leadership practice.

Part I focuses on how great leaders live well and builds the case for frequent reflection, mindfulness, and thoughtful intentionality in leadership.

Self-knowledge is foundational for our effectiveness as leaders, so we'll begin in Chapter One with a focus on self-reflection and explore the question, "Who are you as a leader?" We'll reflect on the critical need for leaders to consider their identity, values, and the legacy they want to leave in their organization.

Often leaders need specific ideas for integrating these habits into their busy lives, and chapter 2 offers practical strategies for developing the will to cultivate these habits of reflection and mindfulness.

Many leaders are challenged with how to manage their time strategically in order to balance self-care with a servant leadership mindset. Chapter 3 presents the concept that time management skills are more than just technical skills; time management means being mindful that we must take the time each day to nurture ourselves in order to serve others as we want to. We can only serve others from a position of strength, and that means managing our time with a laser-like focus each day.

In chapter 4, the focus is on the concept of transitions and how leaders who are deeply grounded in their guiding principles can and should communicate clearly and remain connected with their people when the organization is involved in adaptive change.

This is one of the biggest challenges for leaders today—change is pervasive! Knowledge about leading during transitions can build an awareness of what's happening to our people, as well as what's happening to us as leaders during these times.

With clear guiding principles, Uncommon Leaders lead strong by demonstrating the courage and integrity that are grounded in their values and beliefs.

Part II examines the critical element of trust in organizations and how trust develops when leaders consistently act in alignment with the values and beliefs that guide them.

Chapter 5 focuses on the importance of offering and receiving skillful feedback. Uncommon Leaders shape the culture of the organization by offering positive feedback when behaviors and attitudes are aligned with the leader's vision and by offering constructive feedback when behaviors or attitudes need to be addressed. This chapter offers a strategy for offering feedback and reinforces how feedback is directly related to the trustworthiness of every leader.

Chapters 6 and 7 discuss the importance of having complex, difficult conversations when they're needed and how to prepare for these hard conversations. Skillful preparation can be the difference between hard conversations that go well those that do not.

Finally, Chapter 8 concludes with a final message about the importance of providing a sense of hope and creating a culture of resiliency. Skillful leaders know the importance of lifting up and encouraging those with whom they work and recognize that failure is a part of learning. The Seven Habits of Resilience outlined here can help you forge your strong leadership.

At the end of each chapter, readers will find an invitation to share their ideas, experiences and questions on Twitter at #UncommonLeadership. As an online community of readers begins to support each other, the themes of this book may become even more relevant and helpful. Great ideas come from other practicing leaders, so feel free to join in!

In addition, readers will find a graphic quote featuring a key thought from each chapter in the closing paragraphs. Those who would like to download a free color graphic quote may simply visit Debbie's website, www.LiveWell-LeadStrong.com, and click on "Quotes."

The goal of this book is to help leaders find that "sweet spot," where they are involved and committed to living well and leading strong. It's a place where we find the exemplary leadership that's so needed today! It's a place where people come to work each day to find that they're inspired, valued, and becoming more than they ever thought they could be.

Here's the truth: If you have the will to develop the skill to become a leader like that, astonishing things can happen in your organization.

I

LIVE WELL

Chapter 1

It's Really All about You

Uncommon Leaders Think and Then Act

Recently, students in a graduate course on Leadership, Learning, and Service tackled an assignment meant to stretch their thinking: They were asked to draft a brief statement of purpose for their lives. In just a few words, they were to sum up who they hoped to be as leaders and the legacy they would strive to leave behind. No problem, right? Piece of cake! Not.

What that wise professor did was so important! He insisted that his students—aspiring leaders—slow down, reflect, and think about what really mattered to them, and then state it with clarity. The professor articulated a primary component of Uncommon Leadership: staying mindful, staying grounded, staying sane in this mile-a-minute spin-cycle world.

One student who had spent most of her life as a musician chose as her purpose statement *Live Your Melody, Love Your Harmony*. She shared that being able to "live your melody" is a result of thoughtful reflection about our guiding principles, our values, our beliefs. We cloak ourselves in courage when we're certain of who we are and when we are living out our beliefs daily in an authentic way. Staying true to our own melody means we walk the talk, we're consistent in our actions, and we're trustworthy. Good stuff!

LOVING YOUR HARMONY

"Loving your harmony" is equally important in both our personal and professional lives, and the most skillful leaders consider it so. We have two decades of school data illustrating that teachers are better working together, that synergy is powerful, and that collaboration based on mutual trust and goal-setting is always a part of our best schools. In short, the best educators are working in harmony, aren't they?

Loving our harmony as leaders may mean that we intentionally teach our school community how to manage conflict, how to interact with respect, and how to focus on solving problems rather than assigning blame. Uncommon Leaders model the importance of harmony by thoughtfully responding to criticism or conflict and by acting in ways that demonstrate their inner courage.

On a personal level, leaders who love their harmony maintain their strength by intentionally cultivating relationships and by surrounding themselves with family and dear friends who offer them joy, humor, a listening ear, and an opportunity for authenticity and vulnerability. Uncommon Leaders are well aware of the value of rich relationships with families and friends and they nurture those connections.

Psychologists are more and more certain about the importance of relationships in shaping positive and happy lives. To summarize these ideas very simply, Uncommon Leaders are those who:

- Take time to reflect.
- Know who they are.
- Know what they believe.
- Act on their values and beliefs each day.

In addition, these leaders experience the decreased stress and the increased sense of freedom that come from being deeply grounded in self-knowledge and self-awareness.

BEING TRUE TO SELF

Bill George states in his book *True North*, "Successful leadership takes conscious development and being true to your life story." It follows that Uncommon Leaders know that in order to be true to their life stories, they must dedicate and commit time routinely to developing their own self-awareness and habits of reflection on their values. Simon Sinek tells us that skillful leaders always "start with why." In other words, they have a clear sense of their purpose and mission, and everything they do aligns with that one direction.

In the midst of their busy lives, Uncommon Leaders realize and prioritize what's most important: seeking coherence and alignment between their beliefs and their actions and staying true to who they are. So, they get up a bit early and take time to just think, or they go on a long walk each weekend, or they find a quiet spot in a coffee shop once a week where they write and reflect—all great ideas!

The result of that consistent coherence between a leader's values and a leader's actions is a high level of relational trust in their organizations—that all-important element of effective schools.

SETTING PRIORITIES

In *Overworked and Overwhelmed*, Scott Eblin asserts, "Giving yourself time for unconscious thought is a key component of making effective decisions when there is a large amount of data or a complex problem to solve." Many leaders today need to make a fundamental shift in their thinking and in their identity—a shift away from the death spiral of constant instant reactions, a shift away from their identity as "concierge leaders" trying to give everyone what they need.

That type of reactive rather than proactive lifestyle ends with leaders depleting themselves and serving no one well in the long run. These well-intentioned yet misguided leaders must make a shift *toward* realizing that prioritizing time for self-reflection is really an investment in strong, effective leadership that will stand the test of time.

In *First Things First*, Stephen Covey uses two concepts to describe work in organizations: important work and urgent work. Covey shares that leaders need to spend time in what he calls "Quadrant Two"; they need to do work that is "important, but not urgent." In other words, leaders need to be forward thinkers, focused on the core work of their organization, following that core mission rather than continually putting out the urgent fires that ignite when the mission is lacking.

SPENDING TIME IN QUADRANT TWO

A wise superintendent once shared how he put this Quadrant Two concept into practice. The Uncommon Leader discussed next kept his focus on important work through mindfulness and reflection.

Bert was superintendent of a nineteen-thousand-student school district that had all the challenges of an urban system. Every year, he intentionally prioritized his calendar to spend three days in the fall and three days in the spring on a solitary retreat. He modeled for all of his administrators the value of disconnecting from the tyranny of the urgent and committing time to reflect, write, read, and reconnect with his core values and guiding principles. His legacy of thoughtful leadership, forward thinking, and purposeful action was a gift to everyone with whom he worked.

At his retirement celebration, Bert was surrounded by people who told stories of his trustworthy leadership, his consistency, and his focus on positive relationships, even in a large school district. Members of the community noted the city's strong support for the school system and successful passage of a bond election, allowing schools to be renovated and new schools to be built after years of inattention to facilities.

Bert's leadership was a testament to his strong modeling of integrity and his coherent leadership in which his actions were aligned to his principles.

TAKING INTENTIONAL ACTION

Uncommon Leaders accompany their habit of deep reflection with *intentional action*. Rooted in their self-awareness, they align their work to guiding principles and actions that permeate every aspect of their work. Here's how Beth, one school principal, did just that:

One of Beth's guiding principles was a strong commitment to synergy—her belief that we only get the type of thinking we need in our schools when many minds work together. That principle informed Beth's leadership, giving her a strong sense of urgency that she wanted to help "open up the system" in her school district.

Teachers in her district were just beginning to experience the value of working together in teams, but Beth felt she needed to support that collaboration by structuring teachers' time and availability for team meetings. So, Beth began to transfer her beliefs into intentional action.

First, she quickly realized that arranging a schedule where each grade-level team had their art, music, and PE classes at the same time once a week would provide a needed vehicle to support quality collaboration in every grade.

Beth met with her superintendent and laid out the purpose behind her proposal and a clear "why" for her plan. Collaboration between teachers, Beth explained, was key to doing two things: sharing the best ideas among colleagues and brainstorming ideas when teachers encountered difficulties.

Meeting together during their art, music, or PE time would allow teachers at each grade level to plan curriculum units, develop common assessments, design interventions for struggling students, and support each other so that one quality model of effective instruction was in place in every classroom in the district.

"We want to get away from having those 'islands of 'excellence,'" Beth explained. "This is an opportunity for teachers to learn from the insights and experiences of their grade-level partners."

So, what's the end of the story? Beth put her synergy guiding principle into intentional action, arranging a new schedule for grade-level teams in each school, and outlining a communication plan for everyone involved in order to engage their commitment. By sharing her clear vision for teacher synergy, Beth ensured the fall school schedule began with that foundation laid—a clear "why" for collaborative teacher time.

The important resource of time was provided to support teacher teamwork, and expectations and support were in place for the new model. It's not a surprise that as this collaborative time model developed, teachers felt increasingly motivated and supported and they began looking at their work in a new way. Beth's reflection about the importance of collaboration and synergy had translated into intentional action, and her district—and, most importantly, the students—benefitted.

Beth's frequent practice of reflection about her leadership led her to better awareness of the importance she attached to synergy—that teachers together can accomplish much more than teachers who work in isolation. She then *acted intentionally* on that guiding principle to communicate the value of synergy clearly and to align resources to support that principle.

LEAVING A LEGACY

Beth's story illustrates another point: *The leaders who take the time to reflect on their guiding principles and intentionally act in alignment with those principles are the leaders who leave a legacy in their organizations.* Beth left a legacy of teachers who work collaboratively in a much different way than they had ever done before.

Uncommon Leaders think about decisions with great care, listen actively to others and consider how other viewpoints inform their own, devote time to creative problem solving, and then act on their most-informed thinking. That's the work of leaders who want to leave a legacy in their organizations.

Uncommon Leaders have a sense of urgency about their legacy; they realize they must actively pursue a path that allows them to transfer their values into action. In *A Short Guide to a Happy Life*, Anna Quindlen gently reminds us, "This life is not a dress rehearsal." Looking at life through Quindlen's lens can certainly be a catalyst for change! It's a clear reminder that we all want to live a life of no regrets. Our courage and integrity need to propel us forward now, in the present moment.

Quindlen's phrase offers a sense of professional urgency for leaders. *If we don't take the time to reflect, think, plan, and act today,* when *will we ever do that?* If it's never the right time to assess the coherence between our values and our daily living, then we're in great danger of living a life devoid of meaning and purpose—and of continuing to lead schools that have less and less relevance in the lives of our twenty-first-century learners!

If we believe there's just not enough time to develop clarity about our organizational mission, we're missing a key piece of leadership: consistently modeling and communicating a common vision daily, one that is shared across the entire organization.

It's never been more important to have strong, intentional leaders in our schools, based on principles grounded in what will be best for the young people who are 100 percent of our future. To be clear, we're not talking about heavy strategic plans or school improvement plans written in educationese, stuck in a binder that is never referred to in real life.

Instead, Uncommon Leadership is about a focused sense of direction and mission that helps drive people forward with a force that's unstoppable. That *is* the work right now, and it's the right work that we need to be doing.

So, it's really all about you, and it's about living an Uncommon Leadership life of knowing your values and then translating your values into action. Before you go on, take a look at the strategy for Applying Your Learning for this chapter. You'll find it's a protocol that allows you to think a bit about your leadership formation: How did you become the leader you are today? What are your own true guiding principles? Taking time to jot some notes or journal on the guided questions will form a fine foundation for your next steps.

LOOKING FORWARD

In the next chapter, we'll examine some practical time management strategies for reflection and intentionality. Time management involves taking firm control of ourselves, and it's essential in these busy days. Those ideas will help you to begin living well, developing the habits for the Uncommon Leadership life we all hope for—a life that can truly have lasting positive impact on the schools we serve.

In her 1996 commencement speech at Wellesley, Nora Ephron said, "Above all, be the hero of your own life." That is such a proactive, energy-filled statement! It describes Uncommon Leaders who live well, striving each day to live their own melody, stay true to their own strong purpose, and embrace the harmony of a life well lived.

APPLYING YOUR LEARNING:
WHO STANDS BEHIND YOU IN THE CIRCLE?

All of us come to our leadership roles through our own "leadership formation"; we're the sum of our life experiences, of knowledge we've gleaned

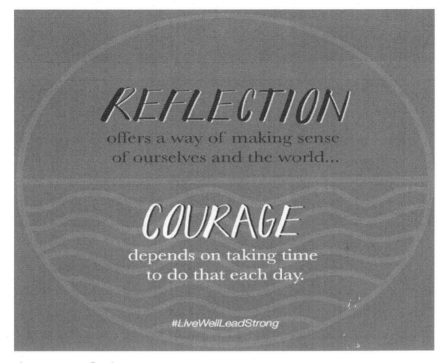

Figure 1.1.   Reflection on Courage

from mentors, and of the values and guiding principles that others have modeled for us and encouraged us to adopt.

This protocol asks you to respond to the simple question: *Who stands behind you in the circle?* Think about and name three people whose influence and impact on your life have formed you into the leader you are and the leader you want to be. Jot notes about what specific elements, practices, or beliefs each of those mentors has contributed to your leadership practice.

Share your thinking at #UncommonLeadership!

Table 1.1.   Who Stands Behind You in the Circle?

This person:	Taught me this life/leadership lesson:

REFERENCES

Covey, Stephen. 1996. *First Things First*. New York: Simon & Schuster.
Eblin, Scott. 2014. *Overworked and Overwhelmed: The Mindfulness Alternative*.
    New York: Wiley.
Ephron, Nora. 1996. Commencement Speech, Wellesley College, Wellesley, MA.
George, Bill. 2007. *True North: Discover Your Authentic Leadership*. San Francisco,
    CA: Jossey-Bass.
Quindlen, Anna. 2000. *A Short Guide to a Happy Life*. New York: Random House.
Sinek, Simon. 2009. *Start with Why*. New York: Penguin.

Chapter 2

So How Am I Supposed to Do This?

The Will to Develop Habits of Reflection and Mindfulness

Okay, my friends, raise your hand if you've had this inner dialogue:

Oh, my gosh! All day long all I did was put out fires and prop other people up! I solved problems and took care of everybody else—the piranhas were circling, and everybody wanted a piece of me! I gave and gave and gave to everybody else. My question now is this: Who's taking care of ME these days?

If you are interested in the power of living well—of stopping the roller coaster and committing to thoughtful reflection as a leader—this chapter is for you. If you're feeling overworked and overwhelmed be assured that, sadly, you're in good company! That sense of drowning is a common malady among school leaders. However, there's hope—you don't have to remain stuck in that spin-cycle!

Well-intentioned leaders often go into their role embracing a true moral purpose—a philosophy of servant leadership. These leaders pave the way, remove obstacles and barriers for people, and pull out all the stops to solve problems and make things happen. Servant leaders focus all their energy and do everything they possibly can to help other people succeed. Their gratification is in seeing other people achieve their goals. Pretty great, huh? Well . . . maybe not.

There is a *dark* side of that servant leadership style. When any aspect of our lives is taken to absolute excess, it can become a negative. Think of the naturally neat person who becomes more concerned with a sparkling house than being present and spending time with friends and family, or the weight-conscious person who nitpicks others' food choices at Thanksgiving dinner.

In the lives of servant leaders, that style of leadership taken to excess actually becomes a *negative* influence on the organization. The two faces of servant leadership are illustrated in table 2.1.

Table 2.1.   The Two Sides of Servant Leadership

Servant Leadership Taken to Excess	*Servant Leadership Balanced with Self-Care*
Teachers and staff become overly dependent and unmotivated. They're thinking, *The 'concierge leader' will take of everything, so why should I bother to help out?*	People see a leader modeling self-care. They work with a leader who prioritizes his or her time and who communicates priorities and values frequently. This leader assigns roles and provides support and accountability for tasks to be done by others.
People may feel resentful and stifled as opportunities for their leadership are rare. Staff turnover is frequent; people don't remain in organizations where they don't feel needed or valued.	People are engaged and motivated because of the opportunities for shared leadership. Staff turnover is infrequent, and a stable environment allows success to be fostered over a long period of time. This leader serves people by cultivating their talents and passions.
Leaders are victims of chronic stress. They often feel depleted and completely worn out because their style of leadership is not sustainable. They begin to resent their work life because they have so little time for life outside of their work.	Leaders intentionally make time for frequent reflection and planning. They believe in and communicate the value of family life, humor, hobbies, friendships, and recreation. They feel energized and model enthusiasm.
These leaders cannot maintain the "leader-centered" school. They go off-track and wind up disappointing themselves, the people they love, and the people with whom they work.	These leaders leave a legacy of shared leadership and systems for common ownership of school initiatives. They have a sense of pride in their leadership and they empower and equip people in their organizations.

THE WILL TO REFLECT

The key message is this: *Skillful leaders develop the will to intentionally adopt habits of self-care in order to be at their most productive. They have an abundance of energy that they focus on thinking about the adaptive, important work—and they do their very best to eliminate as many technical obstacles as possible from their work to help them focus on those "important but not urgent" items.*

Rather than reacting to every problem that arises during the day, Uncommon Leaders take the time to reflect on and to develop systems for solving problems and sharing leadership. They communicate their priorities often, to everyone, and they model calm, principled leadership grounded in reflection and intentionality. Uncommon Leaders seek the important balance between serving others and nurturing their own strength. They know that for their leadership to be sustained, that equilibrium is essential.

So, friends, here's the very real and very important answer to the question, "Who's taking care of me?" YOU need to be taking care of you! Intentionally putting time and energy into self-care is critical to your long-term leadership success and to ensuring you live a life of satisfaction and joy rather than stress and unhappiness.

In this chapter, we'll think about how self-care for leaders must include this commitment—the will—to frequently engage in thoughtful reflection that leads to intentional action. It's called living well!

Trish Allan, writing on her November 10, 2013, mindbodygreen blog, said this:

> There's been a long-held belief that people are worthy of respect only when they put others before themselves. People have often evaluated their own worth (and the degree to which they deserve value in society) by their ability to contribute and place the needs of others before themselves.
>
> Along with this belief is the idea that self-care is self-indulgent. However, we can only sustain physical health and emotional health when self-care is a priority. (This is true for both women and men, despite some old-fashioned gender stereotypes!) When your needs are met, and self-care is a non-negotiable priority, you can come to the world as the best version of yourself; fully nourished and ready to nourish those around you.

Multiple studies over the last two decades have reinforced the importance of self-care in leadership, which includes a commitment to frequent time for reflection. Writing in *The Mindful School Leader*, Valerie Brown and Kirsten Olson share this:

> Research done by clinical psychologists is demonstrating that persistent stress, and being one's own inner critic, compromise our well-being and also activate the body's threat defense system, triggering the release of cortisol and other stress hormones. Self-compassion, on the other hand, supports your goals out of love, not fear. It encourages persistence, which is an important motivational mind-set. (170)

One way of representing the connection between the concepts of self-care and leadership might look like figure 2.1.

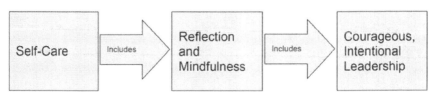

Figure 2.1.   Self-Care and Uncommon Leadership: The Connection

In fact, skillful leadership can never be sustained over a long period of time *without* resting on a foundation of reflection and self-care! For school leaders who are interested in maintaining their courage, their integrity, and their strength through the years, making time for the adaptive work of planning, preventing, and communicating is absolutely essential. It's about coming to the workplace each day in a composed and intentional manner, rather than participating in the "spin-cycle" of urgency that is so compelling.

THE IMPORTANCE OF RELATIONSHIPS

In April 2017, the *Harvard Gazette* reported the results of a unique research study. Scientists began tracking the health of 268 Harvard sophomores in 1938 during the Great Depression, and they tracked this group over *eight decades.* That's phenomenal! The goal of the longitudinal study was to examine clues to leading healthy and happy lives.

The researchers studied the participants' health trajectories and their broader lives, including their triumphs and failures in careers and marriages. The *Harvard Gazette* reports that the findings have produced startling lessons. "The surprising finding is that our relationships and how happy we are in our relationships has a powerful influence on our health," according to Robert Waldinger, director of the study, a psychiatrist at Massachusetts General Hospital and a professor of psychiatry at Harvard Medical School. "Taking care of your body is important, but tending to your relationships is a form of self-care, too. That, I think is the revelation."

Uncommon Leaders have known this truth for a very long time. They tend to nurture relationships by:

- Frequently reflecting on and assessing how they're using their time.
- Watching for the quiet people and encouraging their strengths.
- Being visible throughout the organization often and offering specific praise.
- Encouraging feedback and open dialogue with a focus on listening.

- Balancing their lives and modeling the importance of family and friends—spending time *being present with them,* not *doing endless tasks.*

This commitment to living well has a great deal to do with leaving a legacy of care for those in our organization each day. Our hyperactive culture may not seem to reinforce or value that, but Uncommon Leaders know what is true! When you follow your inner heart, honor your values each day, and adhere to your moral purpose, what does that look like in your life?

LOOKING FORWARD

In chapter 3, we will look at specific ideas for *how* to incorporate this kind of mindfulness into your leadership. Before you go on, though, please take a look at the next protocol for Applying Your Learning. Guiding questions are provided for you to think about refining your leadership vision and the legacy you want to leave. Before we can act as Uncommon Leaders of integrity, we need a level of self-awareness and deep knowledge about our values so that we can act in alignment with them. This protocol is designed to help you in that process.

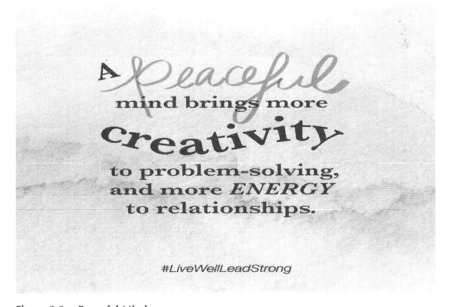

Figure 2.2.   Peaceful Mind

APPLYING YOUR LEARNING:
THINKING ABOUT YOUR LEADERSHIP LEGACY

Table 2.2.   Thinking About Your Leadership Legacy.

What are the qualities of exemplary leaders you've known?
How do you want others to perceive you as a leader?
What legacy of leadership do you want to leave in your school or district?

Share your thinking at #UncommonLeadership!

REFERENCES

Allen, Trish. 2013. "9 Self-Care Essentials to Add to Your Life." mindbodygreen. com. November 10.

Mineo, Liz. 2017. "Good Genes Are Nice, But Joy Is Better." *The Harvard Gazette*, April 11.

Olson, Kirsten, and Brown, Valerie. 2014. *The Mindful School Leader: Practices to Transform Your Leadership and School*. Thousand Oaks, CA: Corwin Press.

Chapter 3

So How Am I Supposed to Do This?

Time Management Strategies for Mindfulness and Reflection

If we believe that skillful leaders commit to practicing self-care through frequent reflection, what exactly does that mean to you, *right now*, in your leadership role? What could you do to form mindful habits that build the inner strength essential for a long and successful career?

For Uncommon Leaders, that strength comes from being grounded in self-awareness about what they value and believe. In this chapter, we'll look at some practical strategies that have helped strong leaders be in touch with their values and then act on them with intention.

TAKING TIME

Surprisingly, the first strategy is very simple but incredibly powerful: Create time for yourself by closing your door each day for just twenty minutes to allow yourself to breathe, think, and recharge. Take that time to read, write a personal note to someone, compose your thoughts for a meeting, and prepare yourself to be purposeful and intentional about your work. Taking control of that small amount of time each day can have a positive effect on your mind-set: You're building your own strength so you can strengthen others!

Dr. Kim Cameron (2012) encourages leaders to cultivate positive leadership by taking a gratitude walk. When you're feeling mired in the muck, take just fifteen minutes to visit spaces all around your building. Don't come back to your office until you've recognized five things you're grateful for at work and given positive encouragement to others. This kind of positive reflection washes back on our own mind-set and helps us remain true to our value of exhibiting warmth and care to others. We build our own strength and creativity that way!

REMOVING DISTRACTIONS

It's also helpful to rid yourself of distractions by turning off your email alerts on your phone. Choose three times each day to respond to emails, and during that time, focus on your messages and give your most thoughtful answers. We live in a culture where we've taken on the stress of needing to respond immediately to any email message. Not only is that unrealistic, but it doesn't serve us well as leaders!

There actually are three very negative consequences of the constant attention to email:

First, responding with an immediate, knee-jerk reaction to every message throughout the day has us typing hurried answers that are sometimes brusque in tone, not as thoughtful or creative as we would like, and not fully responsive to the needs of those with whom we work.

We don't take time to add phrases like "I hope all is well with you" to our email because we want to get the response sent as immediately as possible. We've responded quickly; however, we may have also presented ourselves as uncaring or uninterested in the sender. There are consequences of that that will not serve us well if we value a collaborative culture.

Second, when we don't take time to add the all-important "why" of our response, we leave people wondering about the logic behind our response. We may confirm or deny a request quickly, without bothering to share our reasoning. Trust is reduced when we don't explain our thinking. Uncommon Leaders always articulate their "why"!

Third, each time leaders take their attention away from their present meeting or conversation to quickly type an email response, they're giving a clear and visible message to the person they're with: *I don't value you enough to give you my full attention.* Not very respectful, is it? And it does not align with the message that relationships are a priority.

Instead of trying to respond immediately to all emails, intentionally act in your own best interest. "Chunk" your email time and allow yourself the opportunity to reflect and focus on your communication. Respond to your messages at specific focused times during your day and make every response represent your best self. Remember, every single time you write *anything*, you have an opportunity to represent your leadership values!

Many leaders find the following automatic email response helpful:

In order to support teaching and learning in our school, I regularly leave my office to visit classrooms, observe learning, and participate in team meetings. If you need immediate assistance, please contact my secretary, Monica, at 555-555-5555. Otherwise, I respond to my email at the beginning and end of my day. Thanks for reaching out to me.

Uncommon Leaders search for ways to take firm control of their time, knowing that lessening their stress level allows them to think with the creativity they need. Adopting technology applications that make routine work more efficient relieves the stress of a full inbox. When we free our minds from technical tasks, we have the mental energy to do the more important adaptive work of leadership.

SENDING AND RECEIVING

As they search for ways to streamline their work and improve their effective use of time, many leaders focus on how they send and receive their communications. Two broadly adopted applications are helpful in this regard.

Boomerang for Gmail and RightInBox are email extensions that allow you to write an email and schedule it for sending at a later date. After finishing a meeting, you are able to sit down immediately and write the preview email for the *next* session while the work done that day is fresh in your mind. Then, set the "send later" button so the email is actually sent on any future date you wish. You also can write several routine, repetitive emails at one time and schedule them for the various dates they're needed in the future. It's a great time-saver!

FollowUp.cc allows you to see when a person has opened your email and also allows you to "snooze" email responses, removing them from your inbox and placing them on your calendar to be referred to at a later date when they're relevant. For example, one superintendent wrote, "When you're with us on June 21, let's confirm our dates and get settled for the entire year."

The school principal "snoozed" that email and didn't see it again until it returned to her inbox just before that June 21 session.

Uncommon Leaders don't store and re-read the same items in their inbox for days upon days. Instead, they seek ways to use technology to clear their inbox and free their minds to think about the real work of leadership. That relentless quest to find time each day for reflective work is a daily challenge and using technology for efficiency can help.

THE ABSOLUTE NO LIST

Author Cheryl Richardson makes a strong connection between self-care, time for reflection, and being an effective, balanced leader (2009). In her books,

Richardson suggests a simple but powerful tool she has named "The Absolute No List." She advocates that everyone needs a set of their own life boundaries, a list that they'll adhere to in order to guard their time and energy. For example, on one "Absolute No" list you might see . . .

- I reserve Mondays for days in my office—I absolutely won't accept commitments to lead sessions elsewhere on that day.
- I take time to enjoy my family on Sundays—I absolutely won't spend hours on email or office work that day.
- I absolutely won't rush anywhere in the morning—Instead, I'll get up in time to start my day quietly and thoughtfully.

These are such simple things to do, but adopting your own "Absolute No" guidelines can help you to feel much more composed, unhurried, and grounded as you go about each day.

STAYING POSITIVE

As we've seen, Uncommon Leaders try to take control of their time by using technology strategies for efficiency and by setting boundaries and specific times for responding to emails and adhering to a set of "Absolute No" principles. In addition, thoughtful leaders know that in order to cultivate their inner strength, they need to be vigilant about the negative media messages they allow to "live rent-free in their brain."

Brian, a reflective superintendent, realized that the more often he listened to the network news and checked out social media sites, the more he was affected in a troubling way. Checking out sites online took up valuable time he could have spent in much more important and productive tasks. In addition, the more often Brian checked the media and saw the constant negative messages there, the more his brain was drawn into that focus; he quickly drew patterns of pessimism and anxiety. That's not the person he wanted to be!

Instead, this positive leader decided to limit his time with many media news and online sources and to intentionally stay away from spending much time there. He made a conscious choice to stay engaged with *important* things, limiting his activity to credible news sources. Brian made an intentional choice to fill his mind with positive and creative thoughts instead, and that made a huge difference in his demeanor and presence to others.

Uncommon Leadership involves cultivating that positive, open mind-set that is so important in leadership today! Harvard researcher Shawn Achor, in his TED talk "The Happy Secret to Better Life," states "Our brains at positive function at a much higher level that do our brains at negative, neutral, or stressed. In fact, dopamine, the chemical that floods our brain when we feel happy, actually does something amazing: *it opens our brain for learning.*"

The science of brain research is clear: Only when we're taking good care to cultivate and maintain a positive mind-set will we be able to thoughtfully reflect, creatively solve problems, and productively work with people. Taking time to call a friend, listening to music you enjoy, taking a walk, having coffee with your partner—all of those small life pleasures are really investments in building your strength for leadership. Shift your thinking to view those actions in that way, and you'll begin to truly live well.

The ancient poet Rumi wrote long ago, "Yesterday I was clever and wanted to save the world. Today I am wise and I am changing myself." Instead of constantly feeling that "the piranhas are circling and everyone wants a piece of me," skillful leaders know they must take more control of their lives, must decide to shift their focus to positive, and must take steps to cultivate a balance of self-care that allows for the frequent reflection to replenish their spirit.

Reflective leadership helps us to build strength and leads to intentional action during a long and satisfying leadership journey. The school community in your care needs you to be your very best self—healthy, strong, and positive—so that you can shape your school into a truly wonderful place for learning. Uncommon Leaders can enjoy not only a long and satisfying career, but also a long and satisfying life. Isn't that the legacy we all want to leave?

LOOKING FORWARD

Before you go to chapter 4, do some more thinking about transferring the knowledge about time management in this chapter to your own leadership role. How might you integrate some of these ideas about time management into your practice and commit to living well and leading strong? Remember: Using your time thoughtfully allows you to free your brain from mundane tasks in order to do the important adaptive work of leadership—and that's one key to Uncommon Leadership.

APPLYING YOUR LEARNING:
REFLECTION ON TIME MANAGEMENT

Start with small self-care steps that are manageable and that you can implement with success. The important thing is to get started and maintain your commitment over time!

Share your thinking at #UncommonLeadership!

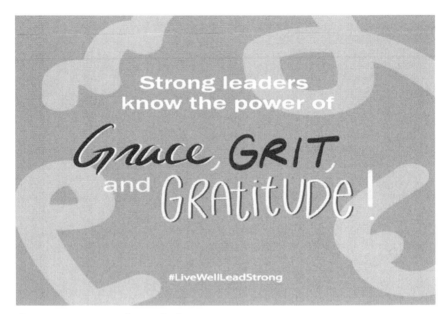

Figure 3.1.　Grace, Grit, Gratitude

Table 3.1.　Reflections on Time Management

My Strategies for Time Management	What Will I Do To Make This Happen, and When?	Who Can I Ask To Support Me?
Chunk my email and close my door for 20 minutes after lunch period.	*Talk to my secretary and give her the reasons for this practice. I'll do it Monday.*	*My secretary and my friend Connie—I'll share this idea with her.*
1.		
2.		
3.		

REFERENCES

Cameron, K. 2012. *Positive Leadership: Strategies for Extraordinary Performance.* San Francisco, CA: Berrett-Koehler Publishers.

Richardson, C. 2009. *The Art of Extreme Self-Care: Transform Your Life One Month at a Time.* Carlsbad, CA: Hay House Publishing.

Chapter 4

Transitions

Where Mindfulness and Courage Meet

All of us have phases in our lives when we're compelled to be the best leaders we can possibly be—times when situations are challenging, when resources are reduced, or when the people with whom we work seem especially difficult. As we think about the root cause of our unease and disequilibrium during those tough days, we should also consider that our difficulty may be a result of some type of transition in our professional lives.

In this chapter, we'll reflect on the concept of transition itself and also discover how Uncommon Leaders can navigate these challenging times well. Leaders who remain mindful and intentional are able to show courage in times of transition, and that's just what's needed as people are staring uncertainty in the face!

Many of us can easily name the kinds of external changes that leaders may encounter: challenges like working with new members on your team, leading a school after two small schools have merged, or moving to an entirely new school or district to take on a new role.

When these external changes occur, Uncommon Leaders know the power of "living well." Their firm grasp of their guiding principles will enable them to travel through transitional phases of their lives more easily than most.

LEADING THROUGH UNCERTAIN TIMES

Calm, consistent leaders can maintain courage and integrity as they lead their team through anxious, uncertain times. So, how do we do that?

William Bridges wrote the foundational work on transitions in his book *Transitions: Making Sense of Life's Changes* (2004). It's a rich and valuable book because the transition concepts are applicable not only to our professional lives, but also to our personal lives. Having a flexible mind-set and a level of comfort with ambiguity can be key to traveling through these changing times successfully.

You might begin by asking yourself: "How comfortable am I with adjusting to new situations and having a level of some uncertainty in my life?" If your answer is "Not very comfortable at all!" you're not alone! But here's what Uncommon Leaders realize: Traveling successfully through times of transition calls for a very flexible mind-set, so intentionally cultivating that flexibility is a great place to start. Begin by developing an awareness of your own "flexibility quotient."

To do so, be mindful about how you can take time each day to cultivate a flexible perspective. This is a delicate leadership balance. People need us to be consistent in our values and beliefs; however, we must often be adaptable to plans as resources, time, and life changes take place. When faced with these types of changes, we can all choose to fuss, complain, bemoan the situation that we can't alter—or we can take stock of our situation and decide what we can control as we continue to move forward.

How do Uncommon Leaders manage times of transition? Three ideas seem important to consider:

1. Leaders must behave in a manner that sustains a high level of productivity in their work, even in changing circumstances.
2. They must sustain a thoughtful, intentional approach to their behavior and decisions.
3. They must maintain a constant awareness of their values and guiding principles so they are trustworthy, consistent, and credible.

When you're under the stress of transition as a leader, it becomes truly important to be aware of those three ideas and to reflect on how you're doing. As the winds of change begin to buffet your organization, holding on to your strong inner self and consistently acting in alignment with your values and beliefs will be a gift to those with whom you work. They'll know who you are and they'll be able to trust in your consistency and integrity.

Many leaders openly communicate with people that "You can count on me for this, and I'll count on you for that." For example, *"You can count on me* to update you twice a week with our timeline and progress for the building project. *I'll count on you* to ask questions if needed and to remain flexible and keep our end goal in mind: a renovated place of learning for our students!" Those two simple phrases assure others that, even though external change is occurring, the values and guiding principles of the leader will remain steady.

Skillful leaders know the power of setting expectations using those two simple phrases in multiple ways!

BEGINNING WITH THE END

Bridges states that there are actually three phases of transition: the ending, the neutral zone, and the new beginning. It may be surprising to think about, but Bridges tells us that transitions really begin with an "ending." Some endings are planned and exciting (think of a son or daughter getting married), and others may be sudden, shocking, and filled with grief.

Many leaders have had to deal with a sudden loss of a staff member or student in their schools, and this calls all of us to be truly at our strongest and most compassionate as we lead through these times.

Many endings, though, are actually a mix of grief as well as gladness—for example, parents may be really happy that their teenagers are "ending" their time as high school students are going to colleges or off to work, but they also experience some feelings of grief and loss related to missing their children when they're gone. (For those of you who are parents of teenagers, that may be hard to believe!)

For our purposes in this chapter, we're going to focus on the important second phase of transition: the neutral zone.

THE NEUTRAL ZONE

The neutral zone is our time between an ending and a new beginning in our lives, and it can be a unique mix: It can be a time of uncertainty, anxiety, and disequilibrium, but it can also give rise to renewed energy, clarity of direction, and fresh enthusiasm for our path. It's all about the choices we make!

For example, principals going to a new school certainly may feel a sense of loss for the relationships established in their first school; however, as they adjust to their new role, they may find new opportunities for leadership growth as well as fresh relationships waiting to be formed. Their intention to remain positive about the opportunity will have a powerful impact on their new team!

Do you begin to see already that your mind-set as a leader will be key to determining how you come through the neutral zone? The choice to remain open to learning during transitions and to intentionally cultivate hopefulness and positivity are key elements of success, and guess what? Those things are totally under your control!

If we consider the word *change* to refer to external issues such as moving to a new town or joining a new leadership team, we can use *transition* to refer to the accompanying emotional and psychological issues that accompany that external change, as Bridges does. For example, if you're a superintendent or principal moving to a new school district, that would be called an external *change*. But the *transition* accompanying that change involves how you actually feel about your acceptance in the new group, whether you feel confident about your capacity for the new job, your speculation on whether you'll meet the expectations for the position, and so on.

As we go through the uncertainty of the neutral zone, it's so necessary to know who we truly are, what we believe in, and how to act in alignment with our values! Uncommon Leaders not only engage in that kind of reflection and intentionality each day, but they see transitions as an opportunity to demonstrate their courage and integrity as leaders. As the ground shifts beneath us in our organizations, leaders who consistently demonstrate their own truth and act on their guiding principles help others know that there are unwavering values that will remain in place no matter what the situation may be.

Cultivating mindfulness during times of transition can be especially beneficial for leaders—in fact, it's essential. People are simply drawn to leaders who calmly listen actively, who seek to understand the feelings of others, and who are thoughtful rather than reactive.

A calm spirit and empathy allow leaders to be actively present in the moment and helps them discern what might be motivating or discouraging others in their organization. Mindfulness results in thinking deeply rather than on a shallow level, and that's essential for successful leaders.

As mindful leaders move through the neutral zone, they focus on consistent, frequent communication with people through multiple avenues. They know that a lack of information and the fear of the unknown can sow distrust, negatively affecting morale and climate in their organization. Most importantly, the core work of schools is about teaching and learning, and distrust and uncertainty distract from that focus!

To circumvent these negative effects, skillful leaders use everything from frequent personal conversations to weekly bulletins, blogs, and multiple social media platforms as well as phone calls and emails to share information. These leaders embrace openness and accessibility and encourage teachers to use a variety of methods to communicate to parent communities also. Today's parents are accustomed to receiving communication in several ways, and effective schools are using creative ideas and technology to forge strong connections.

Trust in the organization is nurtured as people note that information from the leader is true as well as timely. Sometimes it's simply appropriate to say something such as "I don't have all the details on this yet, but here's what I do know now. I'll let you know immediately when I have more information." You've acknowledged that people want information and that you're trying to meet that need.

The neutral zone is a key time for leaders to be visible in the life of their school community and to make as many personal connections as possible each day. In that way, they can gauge how people are feeling and build a network of information and support. Uncommon Leaders make a commitment to be visible and to interact with teachers, staff, and students as often as they possibly can during times of transition—they know that person-to-person interactions are most important when people have questions or need support.

We cloak ourselves in courage. When tough decisions need to be made, people trust that we can and will explain the "why" of the decision and that we'll have solid reasoning behind that decision. Our approachability, warmth, and collegiality should always be evident to everyone, but these qualities are particularly important during the neutral zone phase.

As we lead our group through this time of transition, how do we then move forward into the new beginning? Authors such as Brené Brown and Shawn Achor have written about the power of resilience and positivity as we focus on the future—in fact, our social support system and our commitment to a positive mind-set have a great deal to do with whether we travel through transitions well.

Summarizing an interview with Emma Seppala, Jessica Lahey (2016) reports the researcher's view that "happiness is not something we can afford to lose at home or in our classrooms, as it forms the very foundation of deep, meaningful learning." That makes great sense, as all of us know that when our brains are stuck in fear, stress, or anxiety, we're unable to access the frontal lobe where our executive function takes place. If our schools are truly focused on their core work of learning, then it becomes critical for leaders to reduce fear and anxiety during transitions and to focus on communication and connection each day.

PUTTING IT IN PRACTICE

A great example of a neutral zone in school leadership is related to teacher evaluation. As districts have adopted high-stakes procedures, fear and high anxiety for teachers is clearly related to this transition to new practices. The climate of adult fear that pervades some of our schools is a barrier to student learning, as teachers feel judged, ranked, sorted, and selected instead of supported and encouraged.

Here's the good news, though: We can combat that by intentionally acting to alleviate and diffuse the fear. Uncommon Leaders combat the anxiety by doing things like,

- Making short, frequent mini observations in classrooms so that students and teachers become accustomed to their presence.
- Going to the teacher's classroom to offer feedback rather than meeting in the office.
- Sitting side-by-side with the teacher and completing the evaluation document as a result of the conversation they're having together.
- Focusing on the teacher's capacity to reflect on and be a partner in the conversation.
- Never letting a technology template connected to an evaluation model serve as the most important part of the process. Remember, when we want to help our teachers grow, it's the conversation that counts, not the checklist!

In the neutral zone related to teacher evaluation, approaching a new process with empathy for teachers and respect for their knowledge helps a great deal in terms of reducing fear and alleviating anxiety—and that allows our teachers to perform at their highest levels! If our highest goal is for every student to have an effective teacher in their classroom every day, then it makes great sense to set our teachers up to be successful by focusing on growth in the evaluation process, not on judgment.

It seems that being mindful, intentional, and consistently demonstrating our integrity are the key attributes of Uncommon Leadership during our times of transition. But here's a word of hope for us all: the strategies for leading effectively and courageously are not a secret! They're available for anyone who wants to learn them in order to experience a long and successful career. If you have the will, you can develop the skill to be an Uncommon Leader.

LOOKING FORWARD

In the next section of this book, we'll focus on how to "lead strong." We'll examine what consistent demonstration of courage and integrity looks like and how those attributes can become a part of your own leadership practice. We'll also take a look at how our mindfulness and intentionality form the firm foundation of courage and integrity in leadership and pave the way for a vibrant leadership journey.

Figure 4.1. Act on Your Truth

APPLYING YOUR LEARNING:
THINKING ABOUT YOUR OWN TRANSITION

- Reflect on a whether a "neutral zone" time of transition is occurring for you right now. What strategies for communication and connection will you use to nurture and maintain trust?
- What connections do you make between reflection, intentionality, mindfulness, and transitions? Choose one "first step" strategy to adopt in your professional life that will sustain mindful practices.
- How would you assess your level of comfort with some ambiguity during times of transition, and your flexibility in the face of change? Is it necessary for you to intentionally adopt this mindset in order to be more productive and successful? If so, what will you do?

Share your thinking at #UncommonLeadership!

REFERENCES

Bridges, W. 2004. *Transitions: Making Sense of Life's Changes.* Cambridge, MA: Da Capo Press.

Lahey, J. 2016. "Letting Happiness Flourish in the Classroom." *New York Times*, March 9. https://well.blogs.nytimes.com/2016/03/09/happiness-in-the-classroom/.

II

LEAD STRONG

Chapter 5

The Courage to Offer
Skillful Feedback

In her thought-provoking book *Lean In*, Sheryl Sandberg asks the question, "What would you do if you weren't afraid?" Her simple inquiry resonated with millions of readers, causing people to courageously reflect on their lives through a new lens. For many, that lens included questions like "What are my personal enduring values?" "Is my life a legacy to those values?" "What will I do about it?"

In this chapter, we're going to take Sandberg's question and narrow our thinking. Let's use "What would you do if you weren't afraid?" as a starting point for us to look at our practice of offering rich feedback to the people with whom we work.

As a leader, what would you do if you weren't afraid . . .

- To offer constructive feedback to an experienced, well-connected teacher who is resistant and unwilling to consider your comments?
- To give frequent, authentic, specific praise without caring if people in your school community were accustomed to that or not?
- To address mean-spirited attitudes or behavior on the part of adults?
- To advocate for students when powerful people are making decisions that are not in their best interests?
- To urge teachers to evolve in their instructional practices, and encourage them to consider innovative ideas?

Figure 5.1 is a quick reminder of the model shared in the first part of this book:

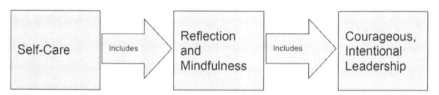

Figure 5.1.   Self-Care and Uncommon Leadership: The Connection

The model paints a picture of this concept: *A commitment to self-care includes prioritizing time for reflection and mindfulness—time away from urgency and pressure. That frequent reflection grounds our decisions and self-awareness; that knowledge about our values and guiding principles spurs the courage we need for skillful leadership.*

POWERFUL FEEDBACK

How do Uncommon Leaders put their values into action each day? In essence, they "walk the talk" of their values in several specific ways.

Skillful leaders offer intentional, encouraging feedback that supports and reinforces the positive behaviors, practices, and attitudes they see in their schools. They know the incredible power of encouragement and the need for people to be noticed, valued, and affirmed. Many leaders routinely keep staff checklists and simple records to ensure that they are connecting with *every* person in the organization in this way. Their positivity is a powerful tool in maintaining the vibrant energy in their organization!

Recently a group of school principals told a terrific story about this: Last June, their superintendent asked every principal, "Who are the unsung heroes in our schools?" Principals were asked to send the superintendent an email outlining who their hero was and the specific reasons their principal held them in such high esteem.

That inspiring superintendent spent the summer writing handwritten notes to each "unsung hero" and mailing the notes to their home address. "You would not believe the tsunami of good will he created in our district," the principals reported. "It truly made our quiet, steady employees feel valued and appreciated. . . . The power of those notes was amazing!" Through a simple act of offering specific encouragement, that school superintendent created a wave of positivity across his entire organization.

COURAGEOUS CONVERSATIONS

There is no doubt that positivity and encouragement are key to skillful leadership. However, as Uncommon Leaders model courage and integrity for their people, they know they also must offer straightforward, specific, constructive feedback when it is warranted. When they see attitudes and behaviors that are *not* aligned with practices that are best for the organization, these leaders step in to offer guidance and direction through specific messages about improving performance.

Skillful leaders are well aware that they must maintain their own trustworthiness by maintaining a clear alignment between their values and their actions, so they don't back away when these interactions are called for. Courage means realizing that conversations may be difficult, but moving forward and holding them anyway.

Exemplary leaders also turn the tables on feedback! They routinely ask for feedback about their own performance, about systems, and about the organizational culture. They demonstrate openness rather than defensiveness and report back to their people about what they've learned from the feedback. Leaders frequently offer feedback, and when they model openness and willingness to receive feedback and learn from it, it's a powerful model for those they lead.

Finally, these leaders plan and hold courageous conversations when warranted. At times, the behavior of those they lead may be severe or chronic, and the person involved may resist constructive feedback. The person may also become a negative force in the organization, so it's essential that leaders address this by planning and holding more complex, longer, difficult conversations. This chapter focuses on skillful feedback; the following chapters will offer information and ideas for these more complex difficult conversations.

PROVIDING CONSTRUCTIVE FEEDBACK

Most leaders are quite comfortable offering encouraging feedback—although, as you'll see soon, they may not be doing it in the most effective way. However, most of us are uncomfortable when we need to confront the dark and murky side of constructive feedback, when we need a person to do things differently or to stop doing something specific that is not in the best interest of our organization.

Why is developing the courage and skill to offer constructive feedback so very important for trustworthy leaders? Bryk and Schneider said it best in one theme of their 2003 groundbreaking study about relational trust in schools: *Trust is demeaned when incompetence is not addressed.*

Think for a moment about the terrific superstar teachers you have in your school district. All of us want those teachers to hold us in high esteem. We want them to be able to say, "Oh, my gosh! We have such a great school! I love it here!" What Bryk and Schneider's study suggests is sobering: When leaders choose *not* to address marginal behavior or performance, they end up disappointing those master teachers whom they most admire.

Most of us want to do everything possible to ensure that our competent, strong, positive teachers are in our corner! When leaders address marginal or ineffective practices, mean-spirited behavior, or other difficult school issues, their master teachers are silently cheering them on. They notice what's happening and they appreciate their leader's integrity.

Strong teachers are grateful for the work their leaders are doing to forge a school where they want to be each day. For those master teachers, and for the students whose education is in your care, you *must* have the courage and integrity to act on what's best for your school and you *must* uphold the high standards to which you aspire. And guess what? It's possible to do, and there are tools to help you.

Like learning to play golf or to master a musical instrument, offering skillful feedback becomes easier with practice. The more we thoughtfully plan and practice what we'd like to say, the more comfortable we'll be when we begin to offer frequent, focused feedback that will impact behavior. When we commit to growing in the area of offering feedback, the skills are easily mastered and have a significant impact on our schools.

A simple but effective model for planning and practicing how to give skillful feedback is available from the Center for Creative Leadership. The SBI model is illustrated in table 5.1.

Table 5.1. SBI Feedback

S—Situation	Name the specific time and place you're referring to. This helps the other person recall the incident. *"In the hallway before second hour . . ."* *"At yesterday's School Improvement meeting . . ."*
B—Behavior	For *encouraging* feedback, name specific, observable behavior you wish to see repeated: *"In the hallway before second hour, **you were greeting every student by name** . . ."* For *constructive* feedback, name specific, observable behavior that needs to change or stop: *"At yesterday's School Improvement meeting, **you interrupted other teachers three separate times and made negative remarks.**"*

I—Impact	The impact packs the power of feedback! It tells the person WHY their actions are important to be noted, the effect their actions have, and on whom.
	*"In the hallway before second hour, you were greeting every student by name. **That personal relationship really sets a positive tone to start their learning.**"*
	*"At yesterday's School Improvement meeting, you interrupted other teachers three separate times and made negative remarks. **When you did that, other members of the team shut down and didn't offer their ideas, so the group didn't work as productively.**"*
	Note: There's no "right or wrong" choice in terms of naming an impact. Most leaders simply choose an impact that they think is most important in their situation.

Original source for SBI Feedback: Center for Creative Leadership, adapted by the author.

Experience is always the best teacher, and as you begin to think and plan feedback, it's helpful to write out your statement before offering it to the person. Several other practical ideas are offered here as well:

TIPS FOR EFFECTIVE FEEDBACK

- *Encouraging feedback* may be given in written form or face-to-face.
- *Constructive feedback must* be given personally. (You might think about this one. Why do you think the face-to-face interaction is so important?)
- It's helpful to go to the other person's classroom or work area to give feedback. Working in that space is more convenient for the other person, it may diffuse a bit of tension, and you have more ability to end the conversation when you wish. (Note: When you plan longer, more complex, difficult conversations, that interaction needs to take place in your office. We'll address that process in chapter 7.)
- Remember, the *impact* holds the power of the statement! Make sure you clearly articulate the *why* of your words. If you refer to just the situation and behavior in your words, you water down the feedback statement; feedback that doesn't address impact is not nearly as meaningful.
- Try not to devalue your feedback statements by saying things like:
  - "It's probably just me, but . . ."
  - "You probably didn't mean to, but . . ."

Beginning your statement with those phrases provides the listener with a ready-made excuse on a silver platter! Do not use "I like the way . . ."

statements. We've *all* said, "I like the way you started class today . . ." but guess what? That statement creates a "leader-centered school" where things begin to revolve around your approval. Feedback is about the other person, not about you. Instead of "I like . . ." try to begin with the words "When you . . ."

Most leaders have had the difficult experience of offering constructive feedback to someone and encountering strong pushback. The receiving person is not open to our feedback and, indeed, is even very resistant or unwilling to consider our words. Just like preparing and practicing to offer both encouraging and constructive feedback, there are strategies and specific phrases you can employ to remain in control of this situation and to maintain your composure.

When you encounter resistance to your feedback the first time, you should simply *repeat the impact statement*. Table 5.2 provides an example for you.

Table 5.2.   Encountering Resistance

Principal to Teacher:	
Situation	"Yesterday, in your 5th hour science class . . ."
Behavior	". . . you used a sarcastic nickname when you called on a student."
Impact	"When you did that, you demeaned the dignity of that student and you modeled bullying behavior that is inappropriate in our school."
Teacher:	
Response	*"That's just my sense of humor! My kids know me . . ."*
Repeat the Impact Statement	"You demeaned the dignity of that student and you modeled bullying behavior that is inappropriate in our school."

When offering these types of constructive feedback statements, leaders sometimes encounter strong resistance and an alarming level of anger. In an intensely charged situation, leaders need some helpful, ready-to-use phrases in their toolbox. Let's revisit the situation in which the principal offers con-

Table 5.3. Dealing with Anger

Principal to Teacher:	
Situation	"Yesterday, in your 5th hour science class . . ."
Behavior	" . . . you used a sarcastic nickname when you called on a student."
Impact	"When you did that, you demeaned the dignity of that student, and you modeled bullying behavior that is inappropriate in our school."
Teacher:	
Response	*"That's just my sense of humor! My kids know me . . ."*
First time:	
Repeat the Impact Statement	"You demeaned the dignity of that student, and you modeled bullying behavior that is inappropriate in our school."
Teacher:	
Angry Response	*"Do you even know how hard I work, or that I have to break up the science content by showing humor with my kids? Do you even know that six kids in that class have IEPs, and they're not really learning anything anyway? Now you expect me not to even joke around!"*
Second time:	
• Add an *introduction*	*"I now have two concerns."*
• Repeat the Impact Statement and add three *statements*.	"As I said, I'm concerned that you demeaned the dignity of that student and you modeled bullying behavior that is inappropriate in our school." *"Now, I'm also concerned with how you're acting during our conversation. I'm not sure what I'll do with my concern. I'm going to think a bit about that. I'll be sure to be in touch within twenty-four hours to talk with you again."*

structive feedback to the teacher who used a sarcastic nickname for a student. The principal states the SBI message and is surprised at the level of anger and defensiveness in the teacher's response. The leader might choose to say something like this, found in table 5.3.

Let's look at those three additional statements. First, the principal put the responsibility for the behavior directly on the teacher—the principal is concerned with *their* behavior. Second, the principal maintained her composure (at least outwardly). Last, the principal has given herself time to cool down, collect her thoughts, call a colleague for support, or research human resource issues if necessary.

In the heat of the moment, there may be a chance that you'll offer a harsh response that will not serve you well in the long term, so give yourself the grace of some time to think about how to respond in a way that affirms your skill as a leader.

Taking that time to step back and cool down is countercultural in our schools, isn't it? Many of us grew up with the idea that strong leaders react immediately and confidently at all times. In truth, our first reaction in these types of situations may not be our best reaction.

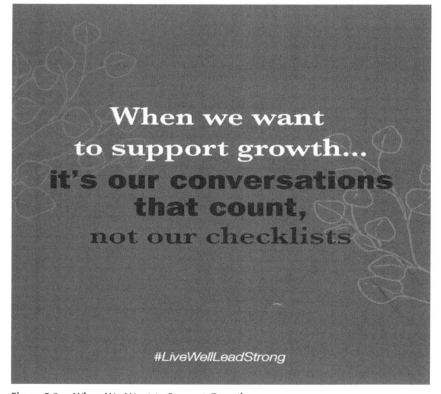

Figure 5.2. When We Want to Support Growth

One leader likened his need for time to think to this life example: Upset with something his teenage daughter said, he hurled the angry knee-jerk response, "You're grounded next weekend! No phone calls! No going out!"

The leader remembers very clearly going into his bedroom that night and whining to his spouse, "Oh, my gosh . . . what have I done? I don't *want* her stuck around the house pouting all weekend with nothing to do! I blew it! There goes our weekend." Oops! His immediate, knee-jerk reaction had results that were unpleasant for his daughter and for him.

Remember: You don't have to respond immediately when someone gets angry. Give yourself some grace and some time to ensure you maintain your poise and composure. After twenty-four hours have passed, the teacher may come back to the conversation in a more reasonable frame of mind. We can all hope for that!

Offering frequent, focused feedback helps us mold our schools into places that reflect our best thinking about learning environments for adults and for students. And guess what? It doesn't cost anything!

Plus, every single intentional conversation we have as leaders is an opportunity for us to courageously model our guiding principles and our core values. That's Uncommon Leadership at its best!

APPLYING YOUR LEARNING: THINKING ABOUT OFFERING FEEDBACK

- Think about the positive behavior of a person you know—behavior you want them to replicate for the good of your school. Craft an encouraging SBI statement and then offer the statement in person or in writing.
- Think about another person's behavior that is not aligned with what's best for your school and that affects others negatively. Write a constructive SBI statement and practice delivering it so that you're speaking in your own tone and feel confident. Then, deliver the feedback, face-to-face with the person. Review the tips for resistance to feedback so you're prepared if that occurs.
- Set a goal of offering specific, encouraging feedback at least three times per week in a handwritten note to someone. Mail it to their home via US mail.
- Set a time to reflect on your process for offering frequent, focused feedback to people. What's going well? What are you learning?

Share your thinking at #UncommonLeadership!

REFERENCES

Bryk, A., and Schneider, B. 2003. Trust in Schools: A Core Resource for School Reform. *Educational Leadership* 60(6): 40–45.

Center for Creative Leadership. 2016. *Feedback That Works: Coach with Conversations*. Greensboro, NC: Center for Creative Leadership.

Sandberg, S. 2013. *Lean in: Women, Work, and the Will to Lead*. New York: Alfred A. Knopf Publishing.

Chapter 6

Difficult Conversations

Let's Not Avoid Them!

Now that you have learned a bit about how to offer skillful feedback, let's move a step further! What happens when a problem is urgent and severe, and you believe that more than a brief feedback statement is warranted? How about when you've offered constructive feedback to someone and the person is repeatedly resistant? What happens when the problem is deeper or more complex than can be managed with just one feedback conversation?

In this chapter, we'll explore why your courage and integrity are especially important in the difficult conversations you hold. This topic may be relevant as you consider a hard conversation about performance evaluation, a sobering conversation with an employee whose performance is not where you want it to be.

Sometimes a difficult conversation may involve sharing some forward planning, requesting that someone teach a different schedule or grade level, work with a different colleague, or adapt to another change. At times, school leaders must also hold these intentional, well-planned conversations with parents, engaging them in a discussion about their students' issues at school.

All these instances call for skillful leadership and provide an opportunity for us to actually live out our guiding principles and values.

CONSIDERING CONVERSATIONS

Before we learn how to thoughtfully plan and hold one of those hard conversations, let's start with two questions: *What are the barriers that* stop *us from holding those difficult conversations? What are the consequences when we* don't *hold them?*

45

Often, leaders know that a conversation is necessary and have an idea of what they must say, but for multiple reasons they sidestep or postpone the conversation. In the end, the problem worsens and the leader's effectiveness is severely damaged.

Let's think about the reasons we back away from these hard discussions and reflect on what an Uncommon Leader would consider:

Reason: "People may not like me—that's a hard thing! Conflict is upsetting and anxiety-producing."

Consider: The most important characteristic people seek in leaders is trust-worthiness—that leaders live out their values and beliefs. That's far more important than likeability. If you hold a conversation in a professional and courteous manner, there's no reason for the experience to be mean-spirited or demeaning. Holding a hard conversation with someone doesn't mean you don't continue to exhibit a caring demeanor—that balance just takes skill and practice. And conflict? The true conflict occurs in our own souls, when we aren't remaining true to who we really aspire to be as exemplary leaders.

Reason: "The person is just having a bad time right now . . . I hope it'll get better."

Consider: Your job as a leader is to advocate for your students. You can exhibit empathy for any of your teachers, but it must be balanced by concern for the quality of what's happening in the classroom for kids each day. One strategy to think about: If a person is struggling with a personal life issue, align colleagues and team members of the struggling teacher to offer their support and share planning and resources on a short-term basis until the person is on a more even keel. But continue to monitor the person frequently, showing empathy while balancing your support with accountability.

Reason: "I'm worried about saying the wrong thing and making the person angry. Plus, this feels hard and I feel isolated and all alone in handling this!"

Consider: Steel yourself; you might get that reaction. Plan your conversation carefully with a trusted partner so you feel prepared. Also think ahead about the possible angry reaction. Brace yourself to remain calm, your voice and body language professional. Listen carefully to show that you're hearing what the person says. Sometimes we also need to "say what we see." It's okay to calmly state something like, "It seems there's a high level of tension around this. We're going to stop the conversation at this point. I'll be in touch tomorrow to reschedule." That's perfectly appropriate! After the conversation, call your trusted colleague and debrief. All of us need to take care of ourselves when we do this difficult work.

For all the reasons given previously, we may hesitate to hold these hard conversations. Uncommon Leaders simply weigh the consequences carefully and walk through these challenging interactions with their integrity and values intact.

Here's the very sobering question for us all to face as leaders: *What are the consequences when we delay or when we don't hold those difficult conversations?* The research by Bryk and Schneider around relational trust in schools is clear: *Trust erodes when incompetence is not addressed.*

Make no mistake, your competent, strong, positive people are in your corner! They are silently cheering you on when you address issues and forge a school with high standards where they want to work each day. For those fine people and for the students whose education is in your care, you *must* act on what's best for the organization and you *must* uphold the high standards to which you aspire.

CHALLENGING THE PROCESS

Kouzes and Posner tell us in *The Truth about Leadership* that all exemplary leaders *challenge the process.* These leaders are not afraid to ask questions like "What evidence do we have that our current practice is leading to best results for our students?" "Have we considered . . . ?" or "What did you notice about your students during the lesson?"

To challenge the process, Uncommon Leaders may use focused, specific questions such as "What will be your first step in addressing this issue?" or "Where will I find that strategy in your planning for next week?" Skillful questioning allows leaders to calmly assert their authority and firmly hold people accountable when necessary.

Kouzes and Posner also tell us that "challenge is the crucible for greatness"—and that's so true! Although these difficult conversations may be messy and swampy, they are also opportunities for us to be at our best and to leave our legacy of Uncommon Leadership.

The best leaders know that in order to maintain their trustworthiness, they must hold difficult conversations as soon as possible. When we avoid difficult interactions, we suffer the consequences in how people perceive us and our reputations as persons of integrity are damaged. What's more, our own health and well-being are at stake when we avoid these problems! Without question, living in a sustained state of stress and tension can cause depression, anxiety, and anger. All of this influences our physical being—we can literally make ourselves sick!

Instead, Uncommon Leaders develop the will and the skill to live a life of coherent leadership. These leaders experience the sense of calm certainty: They know who they are, they know what they believe, and they act in alignment with those beliefs. They're living strong!

In our next chapter, we'll examine specifically how to plan for these conversations so that we can hold them successfully. When we plan intentionally for these interactions, we can remove that "knowing-doing gap" and become exactly the Uncommon Leaders we need to be.

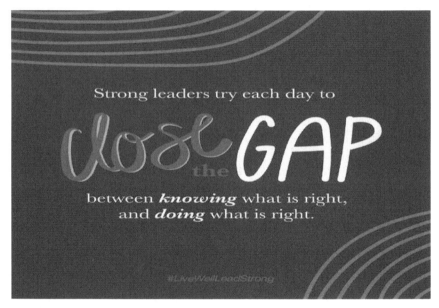

Figure 6.1.   Close the Gap

APPLYING YOUR LEARNING

- Make some time to reflect on an employee whose performance you are concerned about. How long has the problem been present? Have you hesitated or postponed having a conversation? What was your true reason for postponing?
- Who is a support person you could reach out to as you do the work of planning and holding the hard conversation? Take a look at your calendar and set a time to meet.

- If you have an employee who is experiencing difficulty in their personal life, how might you, with his or her permission, help arrange confidential support? Remember, if a teacher is involved, you seek balance: support for the teacher alongside accountability for the quality of instruction the students receive each day.

Share your thinking at #UncommonLeadership!

REFERENCES

Bryk, A., and Schneider, B. 2003. Trust in Schools: A Core Resource for School Reform. *Educational Leadership* 60(6): 40–45.

Kouzes, J., and Posner, B. 2010. *The Truth about Leadership: The No-Fads, Heart-of-the-Matter Facts You Need to Know.* San Francisco, CA: Jossey-Bass.

Chapter 7

Setting Up for Success

Planning for Difficult Conversations

Imagine this scene: A middle school principal named Al witnesses a science teacher using demeaning, sarcastic nicknames with his students. Al uses his Situation—Behavior—Impact (SBI) formula to offer constructive feedback to the teacher; however, the teacher continues to be defiant and resistant to changing the behavior.

In fact, Al soon realizes that the teacher's classroom climate is a barrier to learning: It's punitive, mean-spirited, and anxiety-producing, especially for the students who are most vulnerable. Students' brains are frozen in that kind of environment and learning simply doesn't take place. In a case like this, we, as leaders, must move to the next level and plan a more complex and lengthy difficult conversation.

MAKING PLANS

For help in planning a conversation like this, we'll use three questions and an action: *Why, What, How,* and *Follow-Up.* (I must acknowledge Nancy Colflesh, who taught me this approach as the Purpose—Outcome—Procedure plan based on Total Quality Management.) Table 7.1 illustrates how those questions and actions can help in planning.

What if the teacher wants to bring union representation with them? Two thoughts about that issue:

First, remember that, as the leader, you hold formal authority in these situations. The opportunity for a union representative to attend is simply an opportunity for that person to see a courageous leader in action! So, welcome the person, but set a clear boundary on their role during the meeting.

For example, you might state, "Thank you for being with us today to serve as a listener for Teacher X in this conversation. I want you to understand that this conversation is between Teacher X and me. . . . You are very welcome to take notes and talk with the teacher later; however, your role during this conversation will be as a listener only."

What follows are ideas for framing a memo you can use to plan your conversations. Remember, although none of us enjoys these types of interaction, our courage and integrity as leaders depend on them. So, plan carefully, practice your conversation with a colleague or mentor, keep your WHY–WHAT–HOW–FOLLOW-UP document right in front of you as you speak, breathe deep, and let your courage shine! Your life as an Uncommon Leader is awaiting you, and you're modeling the best qualities of leadership.

Table 7.1. Planning a Difficult Conversation

WHY	WHY does this situation bear this serious attention and what's the bottom-line reason for this conversation to take place?
	Leaders must focus in on a clear purpose and note one over-riding reason for holding the conversation.
	Example: The climate in the science classroom is punitive and mean-spirited and invokes fear in students. This is a barrier to everything we know about the productive climate for learning.
WHAT	WHAT do you want the person to clearly understand at the end of the conversation?
	Here, leaders focus on a few key ideas that the person must take away from the conversation—no more than four or five in one conversation. (If you have more than four or five outcomes to name, you'll need multiple conversations or a more comprehensive Improvement Plan.)
	Example: The key ideas for Al to present to his science teacher are, • *Our school mission includes a caring culture for all students.* • *Multiple examples of sarcasm and mean-spirited humor have been noted and talked about previously—that's not in alignment with who we say we are in our mission.* • *This behavior must stop immediately.* • *A plan must be developed for attention to forging positive, caring relationships with students.* • *The principal will step into the science classroom frequently and will meet frequently with the teacher to monitor progress on the plan.*
HOW	HOW will you best prepare for the conversation? What materials will be helpful to have at your disposal? When and where should the conversation take place?

Example: For Al's conversation, he might prepare by,

- *Notifying the teacher that he needed to meet with him in his office at the end of the day. Two things here: meeting in Al's office gives the teacher a signal that this is a high-stakes conversation and meeting at the end of the day allows the teacher to leave immediately rather than return to the classroom and face students.*
- *Having the office arranged with Al behind his desk and the teacher facing him in a chair, signaling Al's formal authority in this conversation.*
- *Having a copy of the school mission statement available.*
- *Having his log, for reference, noting the previous SBI conversations/dates he had spoken to the teacher.*
- *Having his calendar ready to schedule a follow-up meeting regarding the plan for classroom climate.*

FOLLOW-UP AFTER THE MEETING, what actions does the leader need to ensure take place? This part of the plan is critical because the trust of the leader is at stake: You *must* follow through on your part of the plan for monitoring or meeting with the teacher again.

Example: At the close of the meeting, Al asked the teacher: "What is your understanding of what you need to do now? What questions do you have?"

As the teacher responded that he understood he was to stop his behavior and begin to develop a plan for cultivating positive relationships, Al said, "That's exactly right. So, I'll be stopping in your classroom frequently and I want you to think about formulating your plan with strategies you can use in your classroom to cultivate that positive climate. Which day works for you next week to meet—Thursday or Friday? Bring your first ideas about a plan and we'll work on the final draft together." Al placed the date for the meeting on his calendar and also posted a daily reminder on his calendar to stop into the science classroom.

The last step: Al will use this WHY–WHAT–HOW–FOLLOW-UP template to compose a written memo to email to the science teacher. This provides another signal about the seriousness of this issue and provides needed documentation. The good news? When leaders carefully plan their conversations, such a memo is easily written! They can simply make minor adjustments and frame the memo based on this planning document.

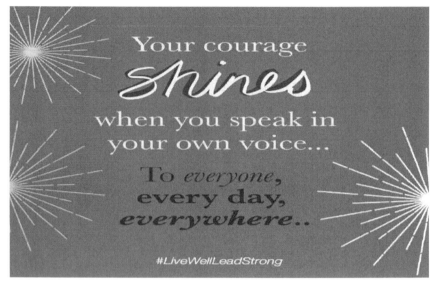

Your courage *Shines* when you speak in your own voice... To *everyone,* **every day,** *everywhere..*

#LiveWellLeadStrong

Figure 7.1.   Your Courage Shines

APPLYING YOUR LEARNING

1. Make time to reflect on a hard conversation you need to have with an employee. Use the template to help you begin writing.
2. Ask a trusted support partner to sit with you as you formulate your thoughts about your conversation. Set a time and place to meet. (Often leaders are hesitant to impose or ask this favor of a colleague. Stop that! If the tables were turned, I'm certain you'd help your colleague, and you will do that at a future date. It's a sign of strength to know when you need assistance—and ask for it!)
3. Start by clarifying the deep reason for this conversation. For example, in Al's case the conversation was not about sarcasm—that was merely a symptom of the issue. The true purpose of the conversation was to address the mean-spirited classroom climate as a barrier to student learning.
4. Make notes about the *What*—the key messages you want the person to hear. Plan to check for understanding at the end of the conversation.
5. Plan the logistics and materials needed for the conversation and contact the employee to set the time and date to meet.
6. Follow-up with your employee as agreed, and also with your support partner.

The following template will help you get started.

Share your thinking at #UncommonLeadership!

Table 7.2.   Template for Planning a Difficult Conversation

WHY: Name a clear, focused purpose for the conversation.	
WHAT: List four to five key messages that are essential for you to convey during the conversation. What do you need the person to know and do? Note: Make sure all your key messages align with the purpose of *this particular* conversation. Use verbs to signify actions the person will need to take.	
HOW: Decide how you'll inform the person of the meeting, the documents you'll need available, the time and place of the meeting, etc.	
FOLLOW-UP: Make note of dates for subsequent meetings, visits to classrooms, promises to provide resources, and so on. Using your notes on this template, construct a memo that recaps the meeting and email it to the person involved.	
REFLECTION: Use this space to think about how the conversation went: what you feel went well and what challenged you. Reflect on this with your support partner who helped you plan the conversation.	

Chapter 8

Strong for the Journey

Seven Steps to Cultivate Resilience

Be honest . . . Don't you wish life was perfect all the time?

Our wish for perfection is so counter to the reality of our daily lives! As leaders, we're often fortunate to achieve goals and celebrate achievements; however, we all have times of disappointment, challenge, difficulty, and sadness. We lose a key school election for well-needed funding, or a vocal parent becomes very critical, a student makes a life-changing mistake, or someone we care for very much disappoints us. We might even disappoint ourselves when we don't feel we're performing as well as we'd like!

This is the reality of the world we live in, and as leaders, we all need tools to push through those times with our strength, courage, and integrity intact. In short, we need to cultivate resilience—what I define as an optimistic nature that allows us to persevere through difficulty and to recover from challenging or traumatic events.

CULTIVATING RESILIENT LEADERSHIP

Particularly in times of challenge, Uncommon Leaders know it's critical to offer optimism and hopefulness, and model resilience of spirit for others. There are seven steps to cultivate this element of resilience in leadership, and this chapter will outline those ideas.

Leadership expert and author Warren Bennis wrote in the January 2007 issue of *American Psychologist*: "I believe that adaptive capacity or resilience is the single most important quality in a leader, or in anyone else for that matter, who hopes to lead a healthy, meaningful life." We all will face difficult challenges; what's important is how we respond to those hard times. So, what do the Uncommon Leaders do?

Leaders who persevere through challenges, who communicate and connect with others, and who maintain their balance when all around them are in disequilibrium will serve their people well. This is the challenging, adaptive work of resilient leadership, and success requires specific steps.

Step One:
BE SMART ENOUGH TO ASK FOR HELP

The most effective leaders lean on mentors, close confidantes, personal counselors, and conversations with other leaders whose insights they value. They read widely from credible authors who share knowledge about their own experiences.

Uncommon Leaders know they're modeling vulnerability and a commitment to learning when they ask for help, and those character attributes are directly related to relational trust. These leaders spend no time or energy covering up, excusing, or being defensive about issues; instead, they wisely face problems head on and consult others to focus on solutions. Isn't that where you want to put your energy?

One superintendent has made asking for help an intentional part of his exemplary leadership practice. Scott meets quarterly with leadership facilitators and retired administrators in two small groups: an Instructional Advisory Group and a Financial Advisory Group.

This superintendent finds the counsel from these outside voices of experience invaluable, and their creative thinking has spurred ideas and solutions in the school district that undoubtedly would not have occurred without their counsel. Scott intentionally takes a risk with the Advisory Groups, authentically sharing information on issues and outlining his challenges, and the team's advice has had a significant impact in the forward progress in his school district.

Just as Uncommon Leaders know the value of seeking assistance with their problems, they also are very aware of the self-talk that goes on in their minds. That leads us to the next step.

Step Two:
BE ON GUARD FOR HARMFUL
MESSAGES THAT LIVE IN OUR HEADS

We must be careful with the amount of shame, guilt, and negativity that we allow to take over our thinking.

Our culture surrounds us with messages that we "aren't enough." We aren't skinny enough, or attractive enough, or wealthy enough, or smart enough.

. . . A constant drip-drip of insecure messages are sent our way every day! Uncommon Leaders know they have to actively counteract that negativity. On the walls of their offices, they display inspirational messages and encouraging quotes as well as beautiful, meaningful pictures. These leaders intentionally read books with helpful and optimistic messages and fill their minds with positivity.

Henry Ford is reported to have said, "Whether you think you can, or you think you can't, you're right." The power of believing in ourselves and viewing life as a learning experience is so important to our success! Uncommon Leaders who remain positive in their self-talk are modeling authenticity and optimism that are vital to creating a culture of learning in their schools.

Step Three:
MAINTAIN A SENSE OF HUMOR
AND SEEK THAT OUT IN OTHERS

Someone said, "An optimist is a person who figures that taking a step backward after forward is not a disaster . . . it's more like a cha-cha." Isn't that humor a great way to lift your spirits? Uncommon Leaders know the power of surrounding themselves with funny messages, humorous movies, jokes, and riddles. They choose deliberately to spend time with people who have a bent toward humor rather than sober pessimists who deflate their spirits and bring them down.

Skillful leaders never use humor in a disrespectful or flippant fashion; they simply cultivate short, funny stories to share in order to lift a cloud of anxiety or unhappiness.

As serious and daunting as times may be, humor can sometimes save the situation from becoming overwhelmingly negative.

Leaders often choose to tell stories that are self-deprecating, growing closer to people as they share their vulnerability. Speaking to an audience of men and women who were making an effort to lead themselves out of serious problems related to poverty, one community leader, Sara, shared her story of playing university basketball. She remembered being so eager to get into her very first game that when the coach called her name to go in, she accidentally pulled off not only her sweatpants, but her uniform pants as well!

The audience heard a funny story, but Sara used the memory to offer a message of resilience also. She shared the humorous side of her life as she also offered a story of hopefulness and success.

People in the audience learned about Sara's "3 Ds": her desire, her drive, and her determination to do well. Hilarity filled the room as she employed the 3 Ds skillfully in her presentation. The result? Every person in the audience that night was left with the message that overcoming a challenge—including poverty—was within their power.

In addition to being smart enough to ask for help, being aware of their self-talk, and cultivating a sense of humor, Uncommon Leaders also practice Step Four.

Step Four:
CULTIVATE A"BIG PICTURE, LONG VIEW" OF OUR LIVES

In doing that, we must realize that our current trials are surely not going to last forever.

One superintendent, Liz, needed to gather her leadership team for a sobering meeting to discuss financial and budgetary issues. She knew her group was going to be anxious about the decisions that needed to be made and she also knew her team was charged with careful stewardship of the district's resources while continuing to engage people in a positive and optimistic environment. Liz talked with her leadership coach, and together they carefully prepared to shape the conversation.

"Always pay attention to planning your meeting before it occurs," her leadership coach said. "It's important to set the physical environment and the tone even before the meeting begins in order to set up people to be successful."

Liz made specific plans to set the stage for a meeting in which people would feel comfortable, valued, and ready to do some challenging thinking. She had coffee and cold water available, and trays of muffins and fruit for people to enjoy. She also had quiet piano music playing in the background before the meeting began.

As her team entered the committee room for their meeting that day, they were surprised and pleased at the thoughtful preparation. Without saying a word, the superintendent had given the explicit message to her team, "We can do this together."

"I know it feels daunting and difficult to look at our finances," Liz began. "You may feel upset and challenged right now, and that's all right. But I want to offer a different perspective. As I look around this room, I feel truly hopeful as I think about the creativity, the wisdom, and the commitment of all of you. My hope for our team is that we'll do our best thinking, resolve these issues, and that sometime in the future we'll look back on these days and simply say, 'That was a really hard time . . . and we went through it all together.'"

That Uncommon Leader had a deep sense of the resilience her team needed in order to avoid getting stuck in the negativity and supposed hopelessness of the financial picture. Instead, she gave her team the clear message that she believed in their abilities. She urged her people to stand together, walk through the present moment, and realize the current situation would not be permanent.

At the end of one faculty meeting where difficult decisions were discussed, a principal, Richard, asked the team to chime in and offer insights from their own experiences. "Before we leave today, let's hear some of your voices and your insights," Richard said. "How do you remain hopeful in your own lives when you're facing significant odds?"

One effervescent teacher spoke up immediately in her own bubbly and positive tone. "I'd like to share my Mom's favorite phrase for hard times," she said. "There are very few things in life that a bubble bath and two Tylenol can't cure!" Her colleagues laughed, but they definitely got the point: Most things look better as time passes and we gain the perspective of hindsight. Uncommon Leaders know the value of taking the long view over time.

Psychologists Richard Tedeschi and Lawrence Calhoun noted a specific resilient attribute in people who have been through difficult times: Instead of being disabled and in a permanent state of suffering and trauma, resilient people have posttraumatic *growth* syndrome. Posttraumatic growth syndrome may take five different forms: finding personal strength, gaining appreciation, forming deep relationships, discovering new meaning in life, and seeing new possibilities, according to Sandberg and Grant, writing in their book *Option B: Facing Adversity.*

Building Resilience, and Finding Joy

Uncommon Leaders know that in order to "live strong," they can intention-ally look for examples of posttraumatic growth and then share stories of hopefulness with others. These stories of recovery and resilience offer power-ful examples and help people realize that life always moves forward and the current challenge will not last forever.

Brian was devastated when he lost his job as a food broker with a large grocery chain. After months of grief and soul-searching, Brian eventually experienced remarkable posttraumatic growth: He took a position with a large nonprofit organization focused on eliminating hunger. In his rewarding new role, Brian drew on his knowledge of the food industry but combined it with his social justice values. He says he'll always look back with amazement at how his job loss turned into a time of incredible life satisfaction for him.

The five forms of posttraumatic growth syndrome are life changing and can provide a way forward for people who are in trauma or crisis. Becoming stronger, cultivating gratitude, being open to deepening relationships, reflect-ing on our own life's mission and meaning, and considering new possibilities are all so important to maintaining resilience! Uncommon Leaders make an intentional choice to be open to this growth, to share stories that illustrate its possibility, and to model it for others.

To maintain their strength and cultivate resilience through tough times, Uncommon Leaders practice Step Five.

Step Five:
MAKE SURE TO REPLENISH OUR *OWN* SPIRIT

We must do that even when the world is in a spin-cycle, or when the piranhas are circling and everyone wants a piece of us! Anxiety and stress clearly inhibit our maximum cognitive functioning, so resilient leaders do their best each day to attend to their heart as well as their mind.

We can only nurture others from a position of spiritual strength. It's important every day to do small things that lift our spirits, even in small ways. Knowing this, resilient leaders might step outside at noon to get a few minutes of fresh air or sip some tea or coffee that warms them and gives them pleasure. When they do those small things that give them comfort, skillful leaders are building themselves up. They know that they're strengthening their own capacity for meeting the challenges each day may hold.

Resilient leaders might also call a friend, take a walk, listen to music they love, work out, and embrace time with their family. They might read uplifting books and stories or surround themselves with soft music and their journal for minutes each morning to start the day mindfully. They focus on gratitude and choose to remember the people in their lives whom they cherish. They reflect on the small incidents of kindness and hope that occur each day and fill their minds with those positive memories.

One Saturday morning, a group of six young women met for coffee. The conversation turned to the adversarial, mean-spirited culture that seems to be developing in some communities. They feared that their own spirits were being affected by all the negativity and the unkind way they observed people treating each other in public.

All these women worked full time outside the home and all had young children, so they did not feel as though they could be active as volunteers, participate in marches, or give a great deal of time to community service. Still, they wondered how they might nurture their own spirits by taking a strong stand for kindness and compassion in their community and by combating the mean-spiritedness in their own way.

Linda spoke up and suggested, "Remember Mother Theresa's saying, 'Not all of us can do great things, but all of us can do small things with great love?' I wonder if we might commit to doing small acts of kindness in the brief interactions we have with people every day. What might that look like?"

The six friends immediately were enthusiastic as they talked together about actions each might take. From that day on, these six young women vowed to intentionally smile and sincerely thank bank tellers, grocery store cashiers, and countless others who crossed their path. They decided to commit random acts of kindness in order to influence others and to keep their own spirits strong.

Every day, these young women met people's eyes and smiled as they made these common connections. As Linda and her friends offered these "small things with great love," they found they brightened the day for people who were not often appreciated. Linda and her friends also nourished their own spirits by taking a stand for kindness and compassion.

What's the real benefit of replenishing your own spirit? Small comforts keep leaders strong and much more able to maintain their effective leadership over time. As we nurture our own inner selves each day, we're also modeling an important truth for our people: Replenishing our spirits gives us the strength to perform well and it's a worthy use of our time.

Step Six:
MAKE A PURPOSEFUL CHOICE TO SET OUR MINDS AT POSITIVE IN ORDER TO PROVIDE STRENGTH FOR OUR PEOPLE

The power of hope and optimism is the key. These leaders are never Pollyannas who insist things are perfect when it's very clear they're not. Instead, they exhibit a growth mind-set each day. Optimistic leaders know the power of the word "yet," so they state things like, "We just haven't solved that problem *yet*." Or, "We don't have the results we'd like *yet*, but we're making plans to solve the issue." They focus on hope for the future!

Many psychologists have offered versions of three important questions that enable us to remain hopeful in times of difficulty. John Schneider shares their perspectives (1996) and the questions are:

1. *What is lost?* This question acknowledges our grief or challenge, rather than just sweeping it under the rug and keeping a stiff upper lip.
2. *What is left?* This question examines our current assets and the elements in our lives we're grateful for in the present moment.
3. *What is possible?* This question focuses on optimism and hopefulness for our future. It allows us to dream and to move forward.

Resilient leaders enable people to remain hopeful by examining each of these questions. As you see, only the first question focuses on the past; the other two questions lead us to concentrate on the presence of positive attributes in the present as well as possibilities for our future. Remaining hopeful helps Uncommon Leaders to live strong—they know the wisdom of embracing that optimistic state of mind.

Step Seven:
PRACTICE INTENTIONAL SELF-CARE

This step to cultivating resilience is actually a compilation of all the previous ideas and it's such a countercultural message in this age!

Many school leaders enter into their role with a servant leader mind-set. That leadership philosophy is effective, but along with service to others, it must include a healthy balance of care for one's self. Many leaders unconsciously accept a message of unhealthy servanthood—they believe their most important role is to take care of others, even at the risk of sublimating their own needs.

These servant leaders get gratification when others succeed, so they spend a great deal of energy removing barriers, accessing resources, coaching others, offering encouragement and support, sharing their insights, as well as making sure all the technical and logistical areas of their schools run well. They face an unbelievable (and often insurmountable) number of tasks each day! Some leaders even become the "concierge" of their organizations, doing everything for everybody.

There's a dark side to that type of unhealthy servant leadership, and it's sobering for leaders to realize: When you're busily focused on doing everything for everyone, you're creating a "leader-centered" school. You're suppressing creativity and not building the capacity and skills of your people. They'll have little or no motivation toward innovation, since the only initiatives that succeed in their schools are the ones you lead. In the meantime, you become more and more depleted, frazzled, and resentful that people aren't feeling ownership in the work. That's not a formula for living strong!

SEEKING BALANCE

Uncommon Leaders balance the importance of serving others with a commitment to take good care of their own physical, emotional, intellectual, and spiritual beings. They seek balance, humor, meaning, and connections in order to sustain their positivity and optimism. That's the way to live a long, sustained career rich with memories of relationships and personal growth!

Bert was the superintendent of a large urban district of twenty thousand students. He modeled this balance of self-care and servant leadership so well!

One day, Joanne, a special education director, finished a meeting with Bert and remarked to her colleague, "Have you ever noticed that every time you meet with Bert you come out feeling stronger and taller?" Stronger and taller. What a lovely phrase to capture that leader's gift for empowering and serving his people well!

Though he was highly committed to serving others, Bert also wisely modeled balance and the necessity for self-care for his central office colleagues. He filled his life with a loving relationship with his wife and children, a vibrant sense of humor, long-term friendships, support for athletics and the arts, and a deep love for the outdoors.

His role as a superintendent didn't define him as a person; he was much more than simply a school leader. For three days every fall and spring, Bert left the school district to stay at a retreat center. "I'm going to sharpen my saw," he told everyone. "I walk in the woods, I read, I write, I listen to music, and most important, I just think for a while. Our job as leaders is always to be looking around the next corner, to be prepared, and I'm spending time thinking about those future issues."

Bert's administrative team benefitted greatly from his time away. He returned rested, focused, and fully ready to lead with creative ideas and purposeful energy.

While many superintendents might consider themselves far too busy to engage in such retreats, when they discount the idea, they're missing a chance to invest in their long-term success. They are in danger of being caught in their whirlwind of busyness, never realizing they're missing the deep human need for reflection, rest, and attention to their own needs. In the end, these types of leaders may find they've become so depleted that they are unhappy in their role.

Leadership expert Frances Hesselbein wrote, "The leader for today and the future will be focused on *how to be*—how to develop quality, character, mind-set, values, principles and courage." Bert modeled for his team his reflection on "how to be," prioritizing self-care in order to live strong for his administrative team and the students they served. Other administrators reflected on the need for balance in their own lives and realized that they, too, desired that kind of life well-lived.

REVISITING THE ABSOLUTE NO LIST

As mentioned in chapter 3, author Cheryl Richardson has written extensively on the importance of self-care and the need for us to strengthen ourselves in order to serve others well. In *The Art of Extreme Self-Care*, she suggests a strategy that's proved helpful for busy school leaders: make their own "Absolute NO List." School leaders have offered examples of their own lists:

- "I absolutely won't rush any more in the morning."
- "I absolutely won't miss my Tuesday night coffee date with my best friend."
- "I absolutely won't spend time with people who routinely complain, gossip, or focus on negativity in their lives."
- "I absolutely won't miss any of my daughter's swim meets in her senior year."

The leaders who practice this simple "absolute NO list" strategy find it gives them so much clarity about who they want to be. Healthy, balanced people create boundaries and guidelines in their lives in order to maintain control and live strong.

The explicit lists paint a picture of the kind of people Uncommon Leaders want to be and how they want to live. Their personal NO list provides them a sense of consistency and certainty in how to respond in stressful situations. They cloak themselves in courage in order to meet those situations and are prepared to do so because they've reflected on their values in advance.

These leaders are ready to respond when confronted with a negative person, or to courteously refuse that request to attend a meeting on the night of their daughter's swim meet. They've already decided that's not in alignment with their values. Uncommon Leaders are living strong in the best sense as they take care of themselves, in order to be joyful and vibrant servants to others.

MAKING THE RIGHT CHOICES

We've examined seven specific steps to cultivate resilience in leadership in this chapter:

1. Be smart enough to ask for help.
2. Be aware of your self-talk.
3. Cultivate a sense of humor and seek it out in others.
4. Keep a perspective on time and know that your current state will not last forever.
5. Replenish your spirit.
6. Remain hopeful.
7. Practice intentional self-care.

Exemplary leaders realize that these resilient practices are key to living well, leading strong, and committing to a life rich with meaning and purpose. The good news is this: Developing the skills to become an Uncommon Leader is a choice that all of us can make. If being an exemplary leader is a desire that lives in your heart, you can nurture and develop the skills for effective leadership.

The world is waiting for you to live well, to know with certainty who you are, what you believe in, and what you value. The people you serve are depending on you to lead strong with courage and integrity. Uncommon Leaders light up the room with their passion for their people and with gratitude for their work. Their light draws in the people around them, and together they are making a difference and shaping the future for their students.

Be guided by your heart, driven by your purpose, committed to your values, and focused on your dreams. Become an Uncommon Leader—one whose legacy of courage and integrity lives on as a gift to the people whose lives you've touched.

Share your thinking at #UncommonLeadership

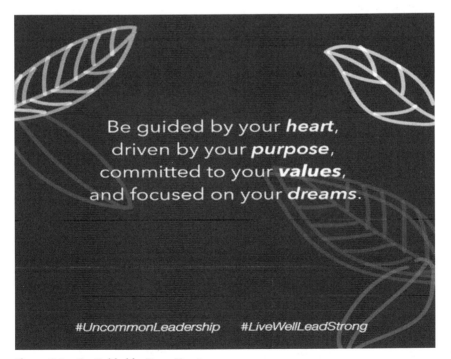

Figure 8.1.   Be Guided by Your Heart

Table 8.1. Applying Your Learning: Your Journey to Resilience.

1. As you think about applying the Seven Steps to Resilience in your own life, which steps resonate with you? Why?
2. As a leader, what particular aspects of resilience do you need to model? How might you do that?
3. In what ways are you guided by your heart, driven by your purpose, committed to your values, and focused on your dreams? How can you take specific actions to live well and lead strong in your own life?

REFERENCES

Bennis, W. 2007. "The Challenges of Leadership in the Modern World." *American Psychologist* 62(1): 2–5.

Hesselbein, F. 2002. *Hesselbein on Leadership*. San Francisco, CA: Jossey-Bass.

Richardson, C. 2012. *The Art of Extreme Self-Care: Transform Your Life One Month at a Time*. Carlsbad, CA: Hay House Publishing.

Sandberg, S., and Grant, A. 2017. *Option B: Facing Adversity, Building Resilience, and Finding Joy*. New York: Alfred Knopf Publishing.

Schneider, J. 1996. "What's Lost, What's Left, What's Possible." The Association for Integrative and Transformative Grief website. integraonline.org/resources/articles/whatslost.htm

Tedeschi, R., and Calhoun, L. 2004. Posttraumatic Growth: Conceptual Foundations and Empirical Evidence. *Psychological Inquiry* 15: 1–18.

About the Author

Dr. Debbie McFalone draws on her experience as a principal and area superintendent to inform her work of empowering and equipping today's educational leaders. Her priority is ongoing, sustained work over time with district leadership teams and educational organizations, as she believes this is how transformational change occurs. Debbie is also a sought-after keynote speaker whose messages focus on the practices of exemplary leadership as well as the importance of resilience, gratitude, and hopefulness.

Debbie holds a PhD in educational leadership from Cardinal Stritch University, Milwaukee, where her dissertation focused on the nature of courage and integrity in exemplary leaders. Debbie equips leaders with relevant and practical leadership strategies, but also helps them develop adaptive skills in areas such as effective decision making, offering skillful feedback, nurturing relational trust, and building highly effective teams.

Debbie is a co-author of the Michigan Elementary and Middle School Principals Association *Leadership Matters* year-long course, and has co-facilitated that intensive learning program since its beginning in 2009. She has presented nationally on the topic of difficult conversations, leads the Instructional Leaders Institute for Michigan ASCD, and has been an adjunct instructor teaching courses on leadership for Michigan State University. Her commitment to educators was acknowledged in a special MEMSPA Leadership Award presented to her in 2017 for her service to hundreds of educational leaders.

Debbie gave the keynote speech recently for the Michigan Association of School Boards summer conference, and has assisted boards with superintendent evaluations. She serves as a leadership coach for numerous superintendents, central office leaders, and principals.

www.LiveWellLeadStrong.com
Twitter: @debbiemcfalone
Instagram: Debbie McFalone